Making Sense of the Ministry

Making Sense of the Ministry

by
Warren W. Wiersbe
and
David Wiersbe

Illustrated by Joe Ragont

MOODY PRESS
CHICAGO

© 1983 by
THE MOODY BIBLE INSTITUTE
OF CHICAGO

All Scripture quotations, unless noted otherwise, are from the *New American Standard Bible,* © 1960, 1962, 1963, 1968, 1971, 1972, 1973, 1975, and 1977 by The Lockman Foundation, and are used by permission.

The use of selected references from various versions of the Bible in this publication does not necessarily imply publisher endorsement of those versions in their entirety.

Library of Congress Cataloging in Publication Data

Wiersbe, Warren W.
  Making sense out of the ministry.

  Bibliography: p. 145
  1. Clergy, Training of.   2. Theology—Study and
teaching.   I. Wiersbe, David W.   II. Title.
BV4020.W48   1983   207'.11   82-20817
ISBN 0-8024-0164-3

2 3 4 5 Printing/GB/Year 87 86 85 84 83

Printed in the United States of America

Dedicated with appreciation to everybody who had a share in our own ministerial training, especially our patient congregations who loved us and endured us while we were learning. We are still learning, so keep praying for us!

Contents

From the Writers to the Reader

Dear Reader:

The purpose of this book is the encouragement and guidance of the ministerial student as he prepares for his life's ministry. Many students are wondering just what relationship exists between their education and their future (or present) ministry, and we want to help clarify that matter. It is our desire to build a bridge between the campus and the local church to help the young minister use the tools he acquired at great sacrifice in school.

We are a father-and-son team. The senior member of the team has been in ministry over thirty years, nearly twenty-five of them in the pastorate. The junior member has been pastoring for six years and, at this writing, is beginning ministry in his second church. It is our plan to approach the topics in this book from the viewpoints of both generations, although we won't always say that. We have discussed these subjects on and off over the years and pretty well understand each other's point of view. It's amazing how much we agree.

We have tried to tie your thinking to the Scriptures, and where we do quote, unless otherwise stated, it will be from the *New American Standard Bible.*

Theologically, we would be considered "conservative" or "evangelical." You may be studying in a school that would not agree with our position, but we trust this book will be helpful to you just the same. In fact, you may need it more than the student in the conservative school!

We have written as men to men. We trust that those women who might read these pages will not brand us as chauvinists.

Each of us appreciates the schooling the Lord has enabled us to receive. Nothing in this book should be construed as a criticism of the schools we attended or the instructors we persecuted. The senior writer has been on the other side of the seminary lectern and knows something of the problems schools face in preparing men for ministry. At any rate, all names have been changed to protect the guilty. The innocent can take care of themselves.

It is our hope that not only the ministerial student, but also the younger pastor in his first church might get help from this book. Also, perhaps some courageous dean might adopt some of these ideas into his school's curriculum. You never can tell what might happen!

Today, it seems a fashionable thing to criticize ministerial training. We are not alarmed; this has been going on for years. Our schools have their weaknesses and limitations, but they also have helped to prepare some mighty servants of God. During the first few years of your ministry, you will be saying, "Why didn't they teach me this in school!" but after you have been on the job a few years, you will probably be saying, "I'm glad they taught me that!"

Both of us believe that the ministry is a great calling. It is not an easy calling, but it is a rewarding one. If what we have shared in these pages helps you enjoy it more and do a better job, we will be happy.

When Archbishop Laud commented on the extreme youth of the "boy wonder" preacher Jeremy Taylor, the lad replied that "it was a fault for which he begged his grace's pardon, but if he lived he would mend it."

Young men are fitter to invent than to judge, fitter for execution than for counsel, fitter for new projects than for settled business.

Francis Bacon

A youth is to be regarded with respect. How do you know that his future will not be equal to our present?

Confucius

A man that is young in years may be old in hours if he have lost no time.

Francis Bacon

Experience is a comb which nature gives us when we are bald.

Chinese proverb

We arrive at the various stages of life quite as novices.

La Rochefoucauld

The denunciation of the young is a necessary part of the hygiene of older people.

Logan Learsall Smith

Don't let anyone think little of you because you are young. Be their ideal; let them follow the way you teach and live; be a pattern for them in your love, your faith, and your clean thoughts.

1 Timothy 4:12 (TLB)*

---

*The Living Bible.

1
The Year of the Amateur

Every pastor could write this chapter, and so could most ex-pastors. The record of that first year in your first church is both exciting and exasperating. In years to come, you will look back at this record with wisdom's smile and maturity's laughter; but while you are writing the record, there will probably be not a few frowns and tears.

One thing is certain: many times you will ask yourself, "Why didn't somebody tell me about this? We never discussed this in class."

That helps to explain why we have written this book.

June 15. I can't believe people are calling me "pastor." I'm not really a pastor; it's just a title right now. I hope I earn it. Made my first official hospital visit today, with a man I didn't know. We chatted, I read Scripture and prayed. It's still awk-ward—he doesn't know me, and yet he's supposed to call me "pastor" and trust me.

June 23. Mowed the backyard at the parsonage, and there are *snakes in my backyard!* (I hope there aren't too many in the church.) The house is shaping up, but I wish the trustees hadn't decided to hang the new doors while we were at the morning worship service. Aren't church officers supposed to attend church?

July 6. I can't believe it! A man in the Sunday school class in-formed all of us that he hears God speak to him *out loud.* When I tried to point out that such an experience was not common, he merely replied that it *should* be. My use of Scripture was a failure; he acknowledges no other authority than what he ex-periences in his life. I'd better meet with the deacons!

July 20. I'm doing a series on 1 John. Preached today about

"Now we know exactly how Nehemiah felt."

testing the spirits. The man who hears God talk (he calls God "the Man up there") informed me that he and his wife are moving to another city. The deacons and I have been praying about him. Thank you, Lord, for solving the problem so painlessly. But maybe now I'd better start praying for the pastor in his next church. I really didn't solve the problem; I just got rid of it. They won't all be that way. . . .

August 12. Our oldest church member had a severe heart attack today. When I went to the hospital, the receptionist wouldn't let me in. I explained that I was the man's pastor, and she said, "You don't look like a pastor." (What is a pastor supposed to look like?) Maybe I should wear a double-breasted suit and carry a big Bible. I finally got up to see him and he was pleased. We prayed together. I felt it was an enriching experience for both of us.

August 15. Expected nothing dramatic at the board meeting this evening; but when I suggested plans for a church choir, they made me feel like I'd committed a mortal sin. I got the impression that they want a preacher, not a pastor who does any leading. I wonder if John Calvin had days like this? Maybe I should start writing a commentary for therapy.

August 17. Met a pastor friend today! Harry serves not far from here and in the same denomination. We met at a hospital luncheon. It made my day! We're getting together for lunch and prayer next week. I wish I had met him sooner. Why don't denominational leaders make some attempts to get fellow pastors together when there's a new man in an area?

August 28. I'm actually looking forward to the fall program. (Am I growing, or just crazy?) One of our young people came home from working at our denomination's camp, and some of her enthusiasm has rubbed off on me. I guess sometimes leaders need encouragement, too.

September 4. I spent a day and a half at our camp and felt it was a real honor to be asked to serve. But one of the deacons said, "If you have any spare time, use it around here. *We* hired you, not the camp." I didn't know I was hired; I thought I was called. Oh, well, count it all joy. . . .

September 6. Bill had another heart attack and went to be with the Lord. I have a funeral to conduct and I don't really know what to do! Did we talk about funerals at school? We probably did, but it was not important to me at the time. Well, it's important now!

September 8. Had the funeral service today. Oh, did I feel incompetent! I didn't know if I should call the deceased by his first name, his last name, or just say "our brother." I felt piously foolish. There sat his family, knowing full well this was my first funeral, and they were wishing I had practiced on somebody else. I don't blame them. I could give them a profound lecture on eschatology, but that wouldn't heal any broken hearts. Even Spurgeon had to start someplace.

October 11. Had a terrific visit with a retired couple who treated me like an adult and didn't once refer to my age. (Most of the neighborhood is still talking about "that new young priest"!) Talking and listening did me good. I felt I was involved in something really important. But not all visits are that way. "What's the preacher doing here?" is the usual attitude. When my professor lectured on visitation ministry, I should have taken better notes. Then again, maybe he didn't say anything worth writing down.

October 13. I've struggled all week with Sunday morning's text and I still don't have a sermon. I have to preach in *two* days. I'm not in a state of panic—*I'm paralyzed!*

October 16. Sunday went great! In my paralysis on Friday, I phoned an older pastor in the area, and he advised me to relax and not struggle. "If you've studied, thought, and prayed, it will bear fruit. Go do something else." So, I went and mowed the lawn (trying to avoid snakes)—and it came! I mean, the whole message just opened up to me. But I'd better not practice this brinkmanship too much. One lady told me the message was just what she needed. She didn't know how much *I* needed it!

November 9. One of our high school couples told me they have to get married. They're worried about how their parents will react. They know they've sinned, but right now the kids need direction and spiritual help, not judgment. I suggested they talk with their parents, and then we'd plan a wedding.

December 2. Working on the annual Christmas program. Lord, how long? The kids have to be bribed to learn their parts, one keeps unplugging the microphone, and one little girl always sings a line behind the rest. (She'll grow up to become an ideal committee member.) Why do parents and grandparents perpetuate this torture on young pastors?

December 12. Thank you, Lord, for giving us a lovely wedding today. The two families struggled, there are wounds, but the healing has begun. The kids are doing well; they'll make it.

I'm seeing more and more that preaching prepares the way for personal ministry, and that personal ministry can help make me a more effective preacher.

December 24. I love the Christmas season. Services were well-attended and the people in a mood for worship. The Sunday school program was a smash hit, in spite of those horrendous rehearsals. Pure grace.

January 14. The post-holiday letdown has struck. Attendance is way down. I think I take these things too personally. Do my sermons bore people? Suddenly, I'm plagued by feelings of self-doubt.

January 27-29. Well, I've made a great discovery: I'm just not cut out to work with high schoolers. I took a group on a snow retreat and did all the planning and promoting and preaching—everything—and it was the worst retreat they ever had. "You can't be all things to all people," my wife said to console me. I feel bad for the young people; they expected more. Another lesson learned the hard way. (Will I ever learn any the *easy* way? Is there an easy way?)

February 15. Day of judgment. My parents and my in-laws were all in church this morning. I was so nervous, I could hardly talk. In the evening it went much better. I realized during the afternoon that God is *always* there, to hear and to bless; so why get upset about people?

March 1-10. Vacation! Just the two of us and no phones ringing. Gloria says she doesn't want to be a "leader" in the church, just a help and an encouragement to me. She's right, but some of the ladies won't like it. They want her to do everything so they can do nothing.

March 29. I made a statement in prayer meeting that was evidently misunderstood by one of the families. Of course, they didn't come to me; the word filtered through the grapevine, and it was sour by the time it got to me. So, I boldly visited them this evening and tried to calm the troubled waters. Why do people get so worked up over little things, yet never get concerned about the big things that count, like trying to reach this area with the gospel?

April 11. Well, it came today: I've got to decide about the big question of remarrying divorced people. Sure, we discussed all of that *theoretically* in school, but now I'm dealing with real people and real emotions. I can't let sentiment control; I'll have to go by the Word—but *which* interpretation? Every book I read has a different slant. I don't want to get a reputation for being a "marrying Sam" in this city. Call the deacons; talk; pray.

April 30. What do you say to parents whose son has died? We cried, prayed, cried some more. I guess just being there with them did more good than trying to explain something I really don't understand myself. So many hopes and dreams shattered. I see that I need to keep myself in best shape spiritually, and every other way. I never know when a crisis will hit.

May 4. Reread a textbook on pastoral work. The author tells me to make four visits a day, and the church will grow. Good grief! When am I supposed to study and meditate? Do I dare spend time with my wife? How about weeding the garden and washing the car? This book makes me feel guilty for taking a day off! And what about those persistent emergencies that come to my members' lives at the most inconvenient times? I wonder if the author ever pastored a church.

May 15. Harry and I got a local ministerium off the ground today. We've enjoyed each other so much that we felt we ought to expand the fellowship. About ten of us met, ate, talked, honestly shared needs, and prayed. It was one of the most refreshing, encouraging times I've had in a long while. Pastors need each other, but we all face the same problem: time.

May 20. So, that's what an annual business meeting is all about! I'm thankful it's only once a year! Everybody has an idea on where to spend money. Everybody has a project or a missionary friend. We finally made some decisions, but some people were hurt. But if we give money to every group that sends us a "gimme" letter, we'd never pay the heat and light. How do I go about setting up some policies so we don't have to fight these battles month after month? However, I did learn one important lesson: the pastor and his members learn a lot about each other during business meetings. Wow!

May 23. Well, some of the people who were hurt told me they're going to leave the church. There's a bigger church in the area that is out to grab everybody they can bribe or kidnap, and they've been bribed. Well, so be it. I don't want anybody to stay who is unhappy, but it does hurt my ego. I guess every pastor wants to attract people, not repel them, But I still think our decisions were right, and that's what counts.

May 31. Today I complete my first year in the pastorate. I wish I had paid better attention in school, and that school had paid more attention to the church. Some people got saved; I wish there had been more, but the Lord knows. I had two funerals, three weddings, and lots of committee meetings. I made a lot of visits and wonder what some of them accomplished. I visited in seven different hospitals. I'm beginning to see that my job is to equip others to get the job done. Gloria and I have had to buck some traditions to be ourselves and do the work the Lord called us to do the way He wants us to do it. Whenever I get discouraged, she reminds me: "God isn't judging you on the basis of what other pastors are doing, but on the basis of what you're doing with what He's given you." Bless her!

Nobody said anything about this being our first anniversary at the church. This makes me a prophet! I'm now *officially* without honor in my own country! Count it all joy. . . .

Only the educated are free.

Epictetus

We can get along without burgermasters, princes, and noblemen, but we can't do without schools, for they must rule the world.

Martin Luther

What we call education and culture is for the most part nothing but the substitution of reading for experience, of literature for life, of the obsolete fictitious for the contemporary real.

George Bernard Shaw

The bookful blockhead, ignorantly read,
With loads of learned lumber in his head.

Alexander Pope

Sixty years ago, I knew everything; now I know nothing; education is a progressive discovery of our own ignorance.

Will Durant

Knowledge makes arrogant, but love edifies.

1 Corinthians 8:1

2

What Went Wrong?

Of course, our young pastor's diary could have been expanded to include all sorts of crises and calamities, such as suicides, the recurring visits of the former pastor, the difficulty of turning studies into sermons, and the problem of knowing whether or not we are really doing a good job. But enough has been said to justify the assertion that most, if not all, young ministers have a hard time relating their education and training to the practical work of the ministry. They alternately blame themselves and their professors, and, if they fail to solve the problem, start blaming the Lord. It is then that they start pondering the possibility of leaving the pastoral ministry and serving somewhere else.

The usual explanation from church members is, "Our schools simply don't know how to train pastors!" Educators have been hearing that lament for years and have tried to silence it, but the echoes continue to reverberate. To be sure, there are weaknesses in every educational institution, our Christian schools not excepted. How many times have the alumni said, "Our professors were good men, but they were out of touch with the real church. They tried to equip us on the basis of their memories, not the stark realities of life." One successful pastor told his church that it took him ten years to get over seminary!

This is no easy problem to solve. Where can you find successful pastors who are academically sound, who want to leave the local church to teach in a seminary? And, if you do find such men, how do they maintain their pastoral expertise away from the context of the local church? Ministerial students desperately need role models, but they want the latest models, not the antiques. And not every man who succeeds in the pulpit is necessarily a winner in the classroom.

You must also consider the ever-present problem on every campus of the competition between the "academic" and the

"practical." Most young ministers feel they have received fairly adequate academic preparation, but that their practical training in school was severely limited. Furthermore, too often the various departments confused the issue instead of putting it into balance. "You must spend thirty hours a week on your Greek when you get into a church!" states the Greek professor, and the Hebrew instructor adds, "Plus at least twenty hours on your Hebrew!" (Of course, neither of them has ever pastored a church, so you can't expect them to know how much time is involved in one wedding or funeral, let alone a week's ministry.) The men in the practical theology department just sit in faculty meetings and shake their heads, and they ask the Lord to lead them back into the pastorate.

When the dust settles between the academic and the practical, then the field education department chimes in. "The trouble is that our students don't have enough time for practical service on the field. You don't learn these things just by sitting in classes." We agree, but are there enough churches to go around? Do those churches want student pastors to practice on them? Any sane educator agrees that practical experience and academic learning go together, but it is difficult to maintain the proper balance. The Methodist circuit-riding preacher, Peter Cartwright, used to ridicule the young preachers who had "regularly studied theology in some of the Eastern states, where they manufactured young preachers like they do lettuce in hothouses."

At this point, even geography enters in. The people who need our ministry are located, for the most part, in the cities; but our schools are usually located in the suburbs. (This is not to deny that the suburbanites need ministry.) Unless they live in the city and commute, the students can become isolated from reality and, during their years of study, actually start to believe that what they are experiencing *is* the real world. After graduation, the courageous soldier descends from the ivory tower of his sanctified fortress only to discover, to his amazement, that the world is not like that at all. Worse than that, he soon discovers that he is poorly protected and poorly armed.

We wonder what would happen if our doctors were trained in the same way as our ministers. Granted, the medical schools have their share of teachers who are living on their past, but at least the medical students are confronted with real bodies and real needs. They are not training *for* service; they are training *in* service. They are acquiring skills under the supervision of people who not only know what they are doing themselves, but are actually doing it day after day. The system may not be perfect, but it certainly is way ahead of what we are now doing in our ministerial schools.

Until about 1800, the ministerial student in America studied the same subjects in university as the other students; but after graduation, he moved in with an experienced minister and "read theology" under his supervision. Charles Spurgeon started his famous Pastor's College with one live-in student. Jonathan Edwards was a colleague to his grandfather, Solomon Stoddard, and certainly learned a good deal from him. The mature pastor helped the young student "get it all together," so that the academic and the practical were integrated into a balanced ministry.

When the universities became more "secular," the various denominations began to compete in starting "Christian schools," and that gradually buried the apprenticeship program. A ministerial student could now get his academic *and* professional training in a school. Our modern substitute for the old-fashioned way is the internship program, in which the young minister spends a year or so working with an established pastor. But even that approach has its problems. Not every pastor knows how to work with a younger apprentice, and there are never sufficient churches available to meet the demand.

Students graduate with one of three attitudes toward the ministry: negative, neutral, or confused. The negative feelings often are the result of hearing negative things about the church from professors (or guest speakers) who have had a rough time in the ministry. Obviously, each instructor has different experiences to recall (if he has anything to recall at all), some pleasant and some painful. Teachers with no pastoral experience rarely teach their courses from a local church perspective, so they generate neutral vibrations. It is what they *don't* say that makes the lasting impression. Over the years of his education, the student has to confront these varied impressions, and the result is often confusion. When you add the impressions gained from visiting lecturers, chapel speakers, and senior students who are pastoring churches, it is not difficult to see the problem. Unless those confused impressions are balanced with some kind of positive input, the student will graduate with a rather warped view of the church and the ministry, and he may turn his first pastorate into a battlefield. Or his first pastorate may turn him into a casualty.

As we see it, one of the biggest needs on the campus is the integration of all that the prospective minister studies, so that the ministry makes sense to him. Many schools lack a "holistic" view of ministry. Each department wants to make a lasting contribution, but nobody seems to ask, "How do these academic disciplines relate to each other? What is the total picture?" The student has in his hands the beautiful pieces of a jigsaw puzzle, but he can't seem to put them together—and the faculty may not be much help. As a result, he puts his emphasis on the discipline that interests him the most, or in which he did his best work, and that becomes the center of his life and ministry. It may be theology, Bible languages, counseling, or administration; but, no matter how well he masters that one discipline, he is still carrying on an unbalanced ministry.

So he goes to his first church and sincerely believes that thirty hours each week spent on Hebrew or Greek will make him a success. Or he rests on the fact that his emphasis on Christian education will revolutionize the church and the homes. Or he puts his theology notes in a prominent place on his desk and uses them in the preparation of meaty sermons that answer questions nobody is asking in language nobody can understand. Along come those interruptions and invasions that mark ministerial life, and he finds himself trying to get out of a wilderness, holding only a corner of the map.

Again, we wonder if ministerial training could not learn from medical training. For the most part, the young medical student finds everything in his curriculum related to the care of the human body. He knows _why_ he is in school and what is expected of him after he gets out. He sees some kind of total picture, no matter how vague some of the details might be; and this helps him integrate his studies and experience. Even the specialist begins as a generalist. He has to understand the whole body before he can focus in on his area of expertise. We need specialists in the ministry today, but we all need to begin as general practitioners.

Instead, one pastor takes off on church growth, and another on revising the Christian education program, and a third on expository preaching in the minor prophets. This one spends his time with "small-group ministry," and that one with "one-on-

one discipleship," while another sets up an elaborate visitation program or an expensive "media ministry." All the while, the Body is languishing under the care of worthless physicians who are sincere and dedicated, but who lack a holistic view of ministry and the church. Like the legendary six blind men with their elephant, each pastor is courageously holding on to a part of the ministry but unable to comprehend the whole. And each can *defend* his ministry; for, as Dorothy Sayers wrote, "There's nothing you can't prove if your outlook is only sufficiently limited."

But the schools alone are not to blame. There are other factors involved, not the least of which is the material they must work with. The student has his share of the burden to bear.

"Do you expect us to make giants out of midgets?" ask the educators. "Our students arrive on campus with little or no experience in local churches, and very little knowledge of the Bible. Some found Christ in a secular university while preparing for a different career. Some we have to put into Sunday school to teach them what they should have learned years ago!"

The dean has a different defense. "Times are tough and students have to work to pay their bills. Between studies and jobs, and whatever family life they can squeeze in, they don't have much time for working in churches. Sure, field experience is a part of training; but they can't do everything."

Now a word from the faculty. "Each student is assigned a faculty advisor, and we do our best. But our schedules are as busy as theirs, and we just don't have time for long-term counseling. We can't take every student under our wings for nuturing any more than a pastor could with each of his members. We try, but there are only so many hours in the day." The appointment schedules on most faculty office doors are divided into fifteen-minute segments. Pastors whose churches are located near Christian schools often spend hours counseling students, and those pastors begin to wonder if they are perhaps "unofficial assistant deans"—without salary, of course.

Alas, sometimes the campus does not provide the kind of spiritual enrichment that the ministerial student really needs. If the nourishment is there, the student may not be ready for it or he may not take advantage of it. More than one alumnus has returned to campus and confessed to the president, "I didn't appreciate chapel and campus prayer meetings when I was here; but now that I'm out in the battle, I see how important they were. God often reminds me of things I heard in chapel, and they are a help to me." It's amazing how ideas come alive in the busy marketplace of life. George Santayana said it perfectly: "The great difficulty in education is to get experience out of ideas."

Lack of maturity, lack of spiritual discernment, lack of opportunity for practical experience: all of those plague the student. The struggle to get good grades and maintain a good "campus image" is not always easy. Sometimes the student doesn't really know which courses deserve the most time, and he wastes time on minor classes. Again, he needs perspective; he needs to see the whole picture, to discover where each course fits and where *he* fits. It's better to learn that on campus than to have a rude awakening during your first year of ministry in a church.

However, sometimes the student has the opposite problem: he goes to his first church convinced that he is adequately equipped simply because he passed his courses and got good grades. He thinks he has it made until he discovers that he doesn't know what he's making. Unfortunately, some schools encourage that kind of academic pride: "You are now a _____ graduate!" (Write in the name of your alma mater.) If you want to have an enjoyable hour, page through a stack of Christian magazines and read the school ads. Each school tries to convince the prospective student that he will never make it in the ministry if he attends somewhere else. The ads present pictures of erudite-looking faculty members, or perhaps smiling students. Some schools even dare to name their most famous graduates! (Of course, they never list the duds; advertising costs too much.)

Someone has written, "Education is a man's going forward from cocksure ignorance to thoughtful uncertainty." Even the apostle Paul admitted, "Now I know in part." The young minister who goes into his first church confident that he has all truth in his head may discover that his heart still has a few lessons to learn. It is one thing to know information; it is quite something else to apply it with discernment in specific situations.

To be sure, it is easy for the professor to blame the student and claim that the young pastor simply didn't apply what he had been taught in the classroom; but we wonder if the professor would have done as well in the same situation. More than one professor has taken a church only to flee back to the campus as soon as resignation was respectable. Did anyone really prepare the student for what lay ahead? Did the professor even *know* what lay ahead? Knowing the names of the Hebrew kings will never help a pastor through a board meeting. At the same time, knowing how to prepare an agenda and run a meeting is no substitute for a knowledge of the Bible. What we are calling for is balance.

That leads to another important consideration: often the young minister doesn't know how to evaluate his ministry. He has heard lectures and chapel addresses that talk about "the bottom line" and "where the rubber hits the road"; but, for him, the rubber has hit the bottom line and erased everything. He doesn't know whether he is succeeding or failing; and, before long, he has seasons of self-doubt about his qualifications for ministry. The fact that we live in a pragmatic world, in which statistics are important, makes his situation even worse. Nobody told our young minister friend what D. L. Moody said: "Converts should be weighed as well as counted." The minister is so busy making things work that he doesn't have time to make things last. He feels intimidated by the "superstars" of the ministry, and he starts to avoid pastors' conferences and denominational meetings. He knows there is a book in the Bible called Numbers, but he is more inclined to consider Exodus. He needs to be reassured that the harvest is at the end of the age, not the end of the meeting, and that all annual reports are temporary until the Master reads human hearts at the judgment seat of Christ.

The students and congregations point the finger at the school, and the faculty and administration return the salute. Each excommunicates the other, and that only makes the situation worse. Meanwhile, back at the church, the young minister is excited but confused. What is the relationship between his education and his ministry in the church?

We hope to answer that question to some degree in this book.

If you are now a ministerial student, we trust that these pages will help you make better use of your academic opportunities. If you are a young pastor, we hope we have got to you in time to help you integrate your past training with your present ministry.

To both of you, we say: be encouraged—the ministry is a great calling, and, with God's help, you will make it!

Methods are many,
   Principles are few.
Methods always change,
   Principles never do.

Anonymous

The value of a principle is the number of things it will explain.
Ralph Waldo Emerson

The difference between principles and rules is radical. Rules can be made, and therefore broken. Principles cannot be made, and cannot be broken. Rules are things of time. Principles are matters of eternity. Rules are accidental. Principles are essential.
G. Campbell Morgan

Fasten yourself to the center of your ministry; not to some point on the circumference. The circumference must move when the center moves.

Phillips Brooks

Expedients are for the hour, but principles are for the ages.
Henry Ward Beecher

In matters of principle, stand like a rock; in matters of taste, swim with the current.

Thomas Jefferson

3

Some Principles of Ministry (I)

W hat we want, then, is some unifying center around which we can build our studying and, eventually, our ministering. Like the solar system in which we live, our lives have many planets and moons that must have a central sun or they will collide with each other and bring the whole affair to a crashing conclusion. What shall that center be?

The answer of most people would be, "Success." They say that the student who determines to succeed will somehow keep everything in balance and come out on top. The pastor who wants to succeed will so manage his ministry that others will begin to notice him, and soon he will have it made. *But how do we measure success?* What is "a successful student" or "a successful pastor"? Do we spell the word $UCCE$$, measure things by money? Do we look for numerical growth in the church, or intellectual and spiritual maturity in the student? Can a man be a poor homiletician and still be an effective preacher? Can he be a below-average administrator and still succeed in a church?

We believe that today's "success syndrome" has created more guilt in the ministry than perhaps any other single thing. It has also created problems in our schools. We use the word *success* but really don't define what we are talking about. Furthermore, the success syndrome has enabled some small men to reach some large places, *and remain small.* It has also caused the church to overlook some giants simply because these men refuse to jump on the success bandwagon and join the parade. Walter Savage Landor said it perfectly: "When little men cast long shadows, it is a sign that the sun is setting."

The average denominational leader certainly wants each local church to grow, give more to missions, and cooperate with the folks at headquarters. But some churches are blessed by decreasing; there are "blessed subtractions" as well as "blessed additions." The first few years of a man's ministry in a church may even *create* problems for the powers that be! Success may not always mean sending "good reports" to headquarters. The student who prepares himself for ministry just to fit into a denomination may find himself on a tangent when he ought to be at the center.

It seems to us that the student is training, and the pastor is ministering, so that the local body of believers might mature and stay healthy. Our schools need to teach the prospective minister what the church body is, how it functions, what its dangers and diseases are, and what he must do to help it mature and be strong enough to overcome everything that would attack it. Just as the medical student prepares to minister to the physical body, so the ministerial student must prepare to minister to the spiritual body.

But what about evangelism and missions? What about building a Sunday school or raising a budget? It is our conviction that all of those things are by-products of ministry to the body. When the body is nourished, exercised, cleansed, and equipped through the Word, then there will be serving saints who get things done and help pay the bills. Each local congregation must "work out its own salvation with fear and trembling" as the Spirit directs. Different men will use different methods, but the *principles* of ministry do not change from age to age or from place to place. We care not how successful a church may claim to be or appear to be; if that church is not following the biblical principles of ministry, the whole enterprise will turn to ashes when Jesus puts it through the fire.

Let us, then, suggest some principles of ministry that you should keep in mind as you prepare in the classroom. If you are already in a pastorate, you may want to use these principles to evaluate yourself and your ministry.

THE FOUNDATION OF MINISTRY IS CHARACTER

Any tool that God can use to build your character is an investment in ministry. As Phillips Brooks stated it, preparation for ministry is "nothing less than the making of a man." After all, the work that we do flows out of the life that we live. "Watch over your heart with all diligence, for from it flow the springs of life" (Proverbs 4:23). What the minister *is* is far more important than what he is able to *do,* for what he is gives force to what he does. In the long run, ministry is what we *are* as much as what we *do.*

According to the biblical record, God took time to make men and prepare them for their work. He invested eighty years in Moses! Joseph experienced thirteen years of training before God entrusted him with his ministry. Men like Joshua and David, and even the apostle Paul, had their years of preparation before they enjoyed fruitful ministry. Even our Lord Jesus spent thirty years getting ready for three years of service.

Ministry without character is only religious activity, or possibly religious business. It simply will not last. Henry Martyn wrote in his journal, "Let me be taught that the first great business on earth is the sanctification of my own soul." Selfish? Of course not! Our lives are God's tools and weapons, and we must be at our best if He is to get the work done and the battle won. That explains why the busy student needs to cultivate a "quiet time" each day. Use whatever name for it that you prefer, but the believer's devotional time is a very important part of building character. Spending time meditating on the Bible, praying, and listening to God's voice in the inner recesses of our hearts is the oxygen, food, and water of the inner man. Then, obeying what He tells us is the exercise that helps our spiritual muscles to grow. That is how we build character.

More than one student has experienced a crisis or two during his years of preparation, and those, too, are a part of character-building. Somewhere Luther makes the statement that prayer, meditation, and temptation make the minister; and Luther ought to know! A serious illness, a financial crisis, a death in the home, even a physical breakdown, can be used of God to make us more like the Master. Our first response is usually, "How can I get out of this?" when we ought to be asking, "*What* can I get out of this?" It is then that the student needs to read passages like James 1, Romans 8, 2 Corinthians 1, Isaiah 40, and 1 Peter (the whole letter). He will also want to commune with David in the Psalms.

In the midst of a busy life, you will be tempted to take for granted the spiritual resources around you. It may take an emergency to force you to use them. We can remember times when an unexpected chapel message turned the tide for us. We can also recall occasions when a printed sermon, found in a library book, brought light into the darkness. Whatever you do, please keep in mind that *you* must build character; this means you must avoid anything that would tear down what God is trying to build up. There is no honest way to cheat. There is no successful way to steal. Achieving a good end by a bad means is exactly what Satan wants. We hear of students who plagiarize material, keep library books, cheat on examinations, and who someday expect to be ministers of the Word. It simply will not work.

Financier J. P. Morgan once said that a man's best collateral is his character. It is better to graduate from school poor in the material but rich in spiritual collateral, because God can easily supply your needs when He sees He can trust you. The foundation for your ministry is personal Christian character. If you have that, you have everything. Without it, everything you have is worthless.

THE NATURE OF MINISTRY IS SERVICE

The very word *ministry* is a translation of Greek and Hebrew words that basically mean "to serve others." Our English word comes from the Latin and simply means "a servant." The New Testament world was not impressed by servants. One authority claims that there were over 60,000,000 slaves in the Roman Empire, so why get excited about servants? When Jesus introduced the radical idea that the only way to lead was to serve, even His disciples had a hard time digesting it and putting it into practice. Sad to say, even in our schools, we miss the emphasis that ministers are sevants who lead and leaders who serve. Some of the successful "superstar" leaders in today's church seem to belie this truth, but we believe it just the same. Anything that helps you serve others will also help make you a successful pastor.

Of course, this principle (like all principles) must be seen in its proper perspective; otherwise, the pastor will become an evangelical handyman, hired by a church to do everything from taking people to the supermarket to fixing the church boiler. Paul said it best: "For we do not preach ourselves but Christ Jesus as Lord, and ourselves as your bond-servants for Jesus' sake" (2 Corinthians 4:5). In our lives and ministries, Christ Jesus must be Lord. What we do, we do for *His* sake. There are times when driving someone to the supermarket might be a holy act of service; there are other times when it would be a down-right sin. The pastor needs *the attitude of the servant*, but he must always remember that he serves Christ by serving the church. If he does not serve Christ, he will only hurt the church.

Every gift that you have, every talent, every experience, every phase of training, can be used of God in serving others. If you don't want to serve, then you don't want to be in the ministry. The church today has far too many celebrities and not enough servants. We suffer from what Dr. John R. W. Stott has called "the shameful cult of human personalities." All of us who are called to the ministry need regularly to read Mark 9:32-45, Philippians 2, and Paul's testimony in Acts 20:17-35. And it wouldn't hurt to recall occasionally the penetrating question that God asked Jeremiah's secretary, Baruch: "But you, are you seeking great things for yourself? Do not seek them" (Jeremiah 45:5).

Why are you in school? To learn how to serve. Why are you pastoring a church? To serve God by serving His people. The title "servant of God" is a noble one, carried by such great men as Moses, David, Joshua, and even our Lord Himself. If you have no conscience, and if you are not concerned about future judgment before God, then you can become a self-centered pastor who uses the church to create a comfortable place for himself; and you can forget about serving others. But if you do, please don't call yourself a minister, because in the Bible, a minister is a person who serves others.

THE MOTIVE FOR MINISTRY IS LOVE

Our motives often are mixed, and we don't always know our own hearts. But the best we can, we must cultivate a ministry of love. Anyone who goes into the ministry with any other motive is destined for disappointment and defeat. Certainly nobody would go into the ministry for financial gain! Some might even become ministers to have authority and prestige, or to win the praise of men. It is even possible, like Jonah, to minister simply out of a sense of duty, and not really love either the God who sent us or the people who hear us. That kind of ministry is only drudgery, and it eventually wears a man down.

It is Jacob, not Jonah, who is our role model. "So Jacob served seven years for Rachel and they seemed to him but a few days because of his love for her" (Genesis 29:20). Love and love

alone can transform sacrifice into joy and suffering into glory.
Love motivates us to do our best for Christ and for our people.
Love helps us build people up and not exploit them for our own
selfish purposes. Love enables us to use our gifts and talents as
tools to build with, and not as weapons to fight with. It is love
that helps us to accept criticism and not fight back, or to receive
praise and not get a big head. In short, it is love that glorifies
God; for "God is love."

We not only need a love for God and God's church, but we
also need a love for a lost world. Jesus saw the lost multitudes
and wept over them. We analyze them, categorize them, and talk
about evangelizing them; but we somehow never get around to
it. In our constant quest for "better approaches" to modern sinners, we use no approach at all; and we are like tongue-tied
witnesses who could say the word that would free the prisoner,
but we have other things to talk about first. Andrew Bonar once
asked a guest preacher, "You love to preach, but do you love the
people you preach to?" Too often we approach sinners as
though we are *glad* they are sinners! We are prosecuting at-
torneys instead of witnesses of Christ's love.

During your academic career, beware of a big head and a cold
heart. If the Emmaus experience is any norm for us today, the
mark of an understanding of the Bible is a burning heart, not a
big head. "Knowledge puffs up, but love builds up" (1 Corinthians 8:1, our translation). Phillips puts it this way: "But we
should remember that while knowledge may make a man look
big, it is only love that can make him grow to his full stature."
Knowledge without love is a terrible weapon or a cheap toy,
depending on how you use it. But love without knowledge would
be shallow sentiment, and it could even become undisciplined
lust. We need both knowledge and love, and the greatest of these
is love.

THE MEASURE OF MINISTRY IS SACRIFICE

John Henry Jowett used to say, "Ministry that costs nothing,
accomplishes nothing," Jesus said it better: "For even the Son
of Man did not come to be served, but to serve, and to give His
life a ransom for many" (Mark 10:45). Sacrifice and service go
together, if you have a servant's heart. The true shepherd

sacrifices for the sheep. The hireling hastens to easier pastures.

The example of Bible leaders supports this principle. Moses was willing to die for Israel (Exodus 32:30-35), and Paul was willing to be accursed if it would mean salvation for his Jewish brethren (Romans 9:1-3). In fact, Paul was willing to go to hell for the lost Jews, and willing to stay out of heaven for the sake of the Christians (Philippians 1:19-24)! Time would fail us to speak of Joshua and David, Jeremiah and Nehemiah, Peter and John, all of whom were willing to pay a great price that others might be blessed. Of course, the greatest example of all is our Lord Jesus Christ.

It is a basic law of nature that there must be death before there can be life. The grain of wheat must fall into the ground *and die* before it can bear much fruit (John 12:23-28). There is no neutral territory: we either save our lives, and therefore lose them; or we lose our lives *for His sake,* and thereby save them. That explains why love must be the motivating force of ministry: only love will motivate a person to sacrifice, and even die, for the sake of others.

Of course, the "show-business" approach to ministry these days would smile at such an old-fashioned philosophy. The "new school" of ministry teaches that there is no need to sacrifice, if only you will use the right methods. There are tried-and-proved techniques of success that demand sacrifice on the part of the people, but not on the part of the leaders. Like the Pharisees of old, these "new-school pastors" lay heavy burdens on their people but never lift a finger to assist them. Instead of using their ministry to build their people, these men use their people to build their own personal kingdoms and make them more secure. The only thing they know about sacrifice is how to spell the word.

The sacrifices you make today are investments in your future ministry. If the measure of ministry is sacrifice, then the sacrifices *now* in your life will prepare you for greater sacrifices *then.* If you enter the ministry with the attitude, "Well, how much am I going to get?" you will get just what you ask for. But if you ask, "How much can I give?" then you will get the very best God has planned for you. There are joys in ministry, to be sure; but they are not joys purchased by the sacrifices of others. They are heaven-sent joys that are the fruit of your own private Gethsemanes and Calvaries.

THE AUTHORITY OF MINISTRY IS SUBMISSION

Since Genesis 3, there have been two philosophies in the world: (1) take care of "number one" and walk on other people to accomplish it if you have to; (2) submit to God's authority and expect to be walked on by others on occasion. "You shall be as God" is the gigantic lie that rules the world today, for man is serving the creature and not the Creator. Unfortunately, that satanic philosophy has gotten into the church and brought devastating consequences.

The biblical record seems to indicate that God likes a person to be a servant before he becomes a ruler. Moses and David both took care of sheep—and did their job faithfully—before God entrusted them with the leadership of the Jewish nation. Joseph had dreams of being on a throne, but those dreams would have become nightmares had he not spent thirteen years learning how to serve. If a man is going to give orders, he first ought to learn how to take orders. Nobody should exercise authority who has not first learned how to submit to authority. There lies the essential difference between leadership and dictatorship. Furthermore, every leader ought to serve, if only to know what it means to give account to others; *for every leader is one day going to give account to God.*

Submission, of course, is not subjugation or slavery. To begin with, submission is voluntary, not forced; and it is based on love and trust, not on threats and fear. A subjugated slave loses his individuality and becomes a neutral piece of furniture like all the other slaves. But a submitted servant, yielded to the Lord, *develops his individuality,* grows into the person God planned him to be, and becomes a distinctive tool in the work of God. The person who never learns to submit will, sad to say, never really discover who he is and what it is God wanted him to accomplish.

One evidence of submission, of course, is faithfulness. That has always been God's key to success. "Well done, good and faithful slave; you were faithful with a few things, I will put you in charge of many things, enter into the joy of your master" (Matthew 25:21). "He who is faithful in a very little thing is faithful also in much; and he who is unrighteous in a very little thing is unrighteous also in much" (Luke 16:10).

We cannot emphasize enough the practicality of this principle as it applies to the campus situation. If you are faithful to submit to regulations, to schedules, to authority, you will develop Christian character and the mind and heart of a servant. First a servant, then a ruler. First faithfulness in a *few* things, and then the enjoyment of *many* things. First *toil,* then the *joy* of our Lord. To bypass this principle is to substitute a worldly shortcut and, eventually, destroy your ministry.

There is another test of submission besides faithfulness; that is, how we use our privileges. There are people who can handle responsibilities but fall apart when they are given privileges. Actually, responsibilities are the preparation for privileges; but some people never mature. The immature person uses privileges to help himself; the mature person uses privileges to help others. The careful use of privileges is a mark of a mature person who knows what it means to submit.

James and John wanted the authority without the submission, the privileges without the responsibility. They asked for thrones! But they were unwilling to drink the cup or submit to the baptism. It was perfectly all right for Jesus to do it *for* them, but they would not do it for themselves or for others. They wanted the crown but not the cross, the glory but not the suffering; but the machinery of God's government doesn't work that way. Not even our Savior could reach the throne of glory apart from Calvary, although Satan certainly presented Him with enough alternatives!

Finally, another evidence of submission is a holy unconcern over who is the greatest. A submitted servant is concerned only about the greatness of his master. Apparently the twelve disciples often debated the question of who was the greatest, although we have no record that they issued press releases as the superstars do today. All of us need to take to heart what our Lord told His competing disciples:

"The kings of the Gentiles lord it over them; and those who have authority over them are called 'Benefactors.' But not so with you, but let him who is the greatest among you become as the youngest, and the leader as the servant. For who is greater, the one who reclines at the table, or the one who serves? Is it not the one who reclines at the table? But I am among you as the one who serves." [Luke 22:25-27]

Use your campus years to learn how to submit to authority. It is the only way to learn how to exercise authority.

4

Some Principles of Ministry (II)

THE PURPOSE OF MINISTRY IS THE GLORY OF GOD

This is what helps to make ministry so exciting: we are part of an eternal plan that climaxes with glory, and then continues gloriously forever. Too often, we are shortsighted when it comes to our work. We forget that the purpose of salvation is the glory of God, not just the changing of lives or the mending of broken homes. The evangelist reminds us that Jesus thought of *us* when He died on the cross; but we all need to be reminded that Jesus first thought of His Father's glory. "Father, the hour has come; glorify Thy Son, that the Son may glorify Thee" (John 17:1). Three times in Ephesians 1, Paul affirms that the ultimate purpose of salvation is the praise of God's glory (vv. 6, 12, and 14).

It may be a cliche, but the statement still stands: it makes no difference who gets the credit so long as God gets the glory. "I am the LORD, that is My name; I will not give My glory to another" (Isaiah 42:8). The minister who serves for the glory of God is not distressed by seeming lack of fruit, although certainly he prays and works for a harvest. But he knows that the harvest is at the end of the age, not the end of the meeting or the fiscal year. He is also careful in his own evaluations or in the evaluations of others, because he realizes that only God sees what he is doing and the things that motivate him. "Therefore do not go on passing judgment before the time, but wait until the Lord comes who will both bring to light the things hidden in the darkness and disclose the motives of men's hearts; and then each man's praise will come to him from God" (1 Corinthians 4:5).

We can glorify God by the way we use our bodies (1 Corinthians 6:19-20), by our willingness to suffer for Christ (Philippians 1:19-22), and by our good works (Matthew 5:16). Even our

41

death can glorify God (John 21:18-19). We may not see God glorified immediately by what we do; the glory may not appear until "the day of visitation" (1 Peter 2:22). "By this is My Father glorified, that you bear much fruit." (John 15:8).

The problem is, of course, that not everybody in your church will agree on what it is *specifically* that glorifies God. We do not understand our own motives, let alone the motives of others; and we need to be patient with each other. One group feels that God is glorified when many people walk the aisle. Another group is sure God is glorified by a carefully planned worship service that lifts the spirit heavenward. Others prefer simple worship service that allows for a great deal of silent meditation. Perhaps culture and personal upbringing have something to do with our preferences. But if all of us are determined that God should be glorified, we can be sure He will direct us if we permit Him.

THE TOOLS OF MINISTRY ARE THE WORD OF GOD AND PRAYER

"But we will devote ourselves to prayer, and to the ministry of the word" (Acts 6:4). Peter came to that conclusion after the church faced a near split because a group of widows had been neglected. It is usually the case that church problems arise because those who ought to be ministering cannot do their jobs properly. The apostles were too busy, so the spiritual level of the church went down, and the result was a division. Behind every so-called organizational or material problem in the church is a spiritual problem: somebody is not ministering God's Word and praying as he should.

Some modern books on "success in ministry" have little to say about the Word and prayer. They tell you how to build a mailing list, how to welcome visitors, what kind of parking facilities are needed, and so forth, all of which may have their place but not the most important place. We are cautioned not to preach Bible doctrine in the public services, lest we confuse or offend the unsaved visitors. And yet the early church grew because the leaders majored on praying and preaching. Church history indicates that the high tides of blessing came when God's people prayed and heeded the Word. Many churches today are living on substitutes—perhaps we should say *dying* on substitutes—even though in the eyes of men they are succeeding. We need to heed the words of George MacDonald: "In whatever man does without God, he must fail miserably—or succeed more miserably."

This is a plea for a balanced ministry. If we have all Word and no prayer, we will have light without heat. If we have all prayer and no Word, we will have heat without light. Bishop Handley Moule said he would rather tone down a fanatic than resurrect a corpse, but why must the church be either? A normal, healthy body is what we want! The balanced ministry of God's Word and prayer (and that includes worship, of course) helps to build a balanced spiritual body. Those two tools may not produce the immediate results that dazzle the world, but they do produce the lasting fruit that will glorify God.

During your academic career, learn how to study the Bible and how to share it with others in a way that enables them to understand it and apply it personally. Take every opportunity to hear other men teach and preach. It will take time for you to discover and develop your own gifts, so be patient with yourself. One of the weaknesses of our ministerial training is the lack of opportunities men have for preaching. While preaching in class is better than nothing, it is far from adequate; so use every opportunity you can to share the Word with others. Back up your preaching with your praying. You will use those two spiritual tools for the rest of your life, so learn how to handle them now.

THE PRIVILEGE OF MINISTRY IS GROWTH

Whenever we hear ministers complaining about their calling, we have doubts about their spiritual perception. Every calling has its occupational hazards, and the ministry is no exception. But never lose that sense of wonder that God should choose *you* to be one of His servants! We have the privilege of digging into the Word, feeding His church, winning people to the Savior, and all the while, sharing in spiritual growth ourselves. And we get paid for doing it!

The best part of being a winning athlete is not the prize or the salary; it is the joy of being the kind of person in body and mind who is a winner. Long after the money is spent and the prize forgotten, the athlete has that healthy body, that zest for competition, and that thrill of achievement. What you are, not what you get, is the important thing. No wonder Paul cautioned Timothy, "Take pains with these things; be absorbed in them, so that your progress may be evident to all" (1 Timothy 4:15). That word "progress" means "pioneer advance into new territory." In other words, as the pastor grows in grace and knowledge, the church can grow with him, because he is opening up new territory.

Of course, preachers who don't grow have to move. They use up their file of sermons and their kit of ideas. This is unfortunate, because it is as we stay with the task that we are challenged to grow. If the parable of the pounds teaches anything, it is that faithfulness to use our opportunities always increases our abilities to do more (Luke 19:11-27). Imagine being made the ruler of ten cities just because you knew how to handle money on the market! Faithfulness in that which is little is evidence that we will be faithful in that which is greatest. The man who is faithful to care for his "little flock" can be trusted with more sheep.

We will have more to say about growing in ministry in a later chapter.

THE POWER OF MINISTRY IS THE HOLY SPIRIT

Dr. A. W. Tozer and others have warned us that if the Lord removed the Holy Spirit from this world, much of what we are doing in the church would go right on, *and nobody would know the difference.* Of course, the Holy Spirit works through the Word of God and prayer. Too much ministry today depends on human personality, gimmicks, good public relations, religious entertainment, and various techniques borrowed from the world of show business. We brag about our budgets, but those in the early church had to confess, "I do not possess silver and gold" (Acts 3:6). Our church leaders hobnob with great people, presidents and celebrities, but the early church was persecuted by that same crowd. In New Testament days, the cross was an offense, but today it is part of a success cult.

It was the power of the Spirit that energized the early Christians, and you will need His power for your life and ministry today. Only the Holy Spirit can teach you God's Word and then reproduce God's life in your life. Cultivate the Spirit-filled life by spending time in the Word, praying, yielding, obeying, keeping your life clean, and being available for God to use. If and when you are ordained, that solemn ceremony will not automatically grant you spiritual power. You must cultivate a good relationship with the Holy Spirit now. "The Spirit-filled life is not a special deluxe edition of Christianity," wrote A. W. Tozer. "It is part and parcel of the total plan of God for His people."

You may not see much Spirit-filled ministry on your campus. Some of the faculty and student body may be downright carnal. But that is no excuse for *you* to descend to their level. It might be an opportunity for you to humbly minister to them. Every campus has its percentage of "clowns" who give little evidence of being serious about life, studies, the ministry, or even the things of God. (Some of them may one day be great servants of God, so be patient with them.) Meanwhile, "pay close attention to yourself and to your teaching; persevere in these things; for as you do this you will insure salvation both for yourself and for those who hear you" (1 Timothy 4:16).

THE MODEL FOR MINISTRY IS JESUS CHRIST

Much is being said these days about "role models" for ministry. It would be profitable if each campus could have a resident pastor/preacher of some experience and stature, whose ministry could be an example to follow. That approach has its perils, not the least of which is slavish imitation. Perhaps all young ministers *get their start* by idealizing and imitating some great man of God; but they dare not stay on that course. The imitator never really becomes himself, and, sad to say, he never grows beyond his model.

But when we idealize and imitate Jesus Christ, we become more of what He wants *us* to be, and we grow in ministry. It is not imitation so much as *incarnation*—"Christ lives in me" (Galatians 2:20). There is very little price to pay when you imitate some other preacher; but if you are going to model your ministry after Christ, you must be prepared to sacrifice.

Actually, this principle sums up all the other nine principles.

If the foundation for ministry is character, where could you find a greater character than that of Jesus Christ? Nobody in history surpasses Him! The nature of ministry is service, and Jesus Christ came as a servant. He was God's "Suffering Servant" who made Himself available to all kinds of people to meet all kinds of needs. The motive for ministry is love, and God's love seen in Jesus Christ is beyond our comprehension. *His love for us even took Him to a cross!* Why? Because love always gives, and the measure of ministry is sacrifice.

The authority of ministry is submission, and Jesus Christ humbled Himself and became obedient, even to death. The purpose of ministry is God's glory, and this is what directed Him in His earthly walk. "Father, glorify Thy name" (John 12:28). Jesus used the tools of the Word of God and prayer, and He depended on the power of the Holy Spirit. He even experienced "growth" through His sufferings as He prepared Himself to be our sympathetic High Priest (Hebrews 5:8).

Perhaps the emphasis on the spiritual is not as strong on your campus as it ought to be. That need not hinder you from growing. Joseph was a faithful man even in Egypt, and Daniel kept himself pure in Babylon! It can be done.

We are serving a wonderful Master, and He has called us to a wonderful life of service for His glory. Start now to integrate these principles into your life. They can be as meaningful to a student as to a preacher. Be prepared for some battles, but be assured that God can see you through. The words of David Livingstone, written at the close of his life, remind us of the wonder of ministering for Christ:

> He is the greatest master I have ever known. If there is anyone greater, I do not know him. Jesus Christ is the only master supremely worth serving. He is the only ideal that never loses its inspiration. He is the only friend whose friendship meets every demand. He is the only Savior who can save to the uttermost. We go forth in His name, in His power, and in His Spirit to serve Him.

But this . . . decrees for us in general what the preparation for the ministry is. It must be nothing less than the making of a man. It cannot be the mere training to certain tricks. It cannot be even the furnishing with abundant knowledge. It must be nothing less than the kneading and tempering of a man's whole nature till it becomes of such a consistency and quality as to be capable of transmission.

Phillips Brooks

The Christian ministry is the worst of all trades, but the best of all professions.

John Newton

It is not a minister's wisdom but his conviction which imparts itself to others. Nothing gives life but life. Real flame alone kindles another flame.

F. W. Robertson

Genius is not essential to good preaching, but a live man is.

Austin Phelps

But . . . He who had set me apart, even from my mother's womb, and called me through His grace, was pleased to reveal His Son in me, that I might preach Him among the Gentiles.

Paul, in Galatians 1:15-16

Before I formed you in the womb I knew you, and before you were born I consecrated you; I have appointed you a prophet to the nations. . . . Behold, I have put My words in your mouth.

Jeremiah 1:5, 9

5

Something About Schools

Why go to school to prepare for Christian ministry? Why not just attach yourself to some successful pastor and learn by doing? After all, some of the most famous preachers in history never had any formal training: Charles Spurgeon, G. Campbell Morgan, Dwight L. Moody, and Harry Ironside, to name a few.

Yes, a few—a *very* few, compared to the large number of effective pastors and preachers who *did* have formal training. Furthermore, you must also keep in mind that some of the above-named "greats" sat on school faculties, and two of them (Moody and Spurgeon) founded schools to train ministers. If you *are* a Spurgeon or a Moody, somebody is bound to discover it and perhaps give you permission to drop out of school. Meanwhile, stay with it and complete your education.

But while you are in school, don't make the mistake of thinking that your education by itself will automatically make you a minister. Only you and God, working together, can do that; and it will take some time.

God has many ways of preparing His workers, but He always prepares them. Both Moses and Paul had what we would call "formal schooling" (Acts 7:22 and 22:3). It didn't seem to hinder their ministry too much. In fact, Paul occasionally quoted from the Greek poets when he wrote to the churches. There is some formal preparation that is good for *all* of God's servants, and some preparation that has to be tailor-made. God alone knows the man and the ministry He has in mind for him, and each of us must be sensitive to God's leading. It is when we start convincing ourselves that we are "exceptions" that we will get into trouble.

Strictly speaking, there is a difference between *training* and *education*. Training prepares you to make a living; education prepares you to make a life. Training means enablement, while education means enrichment. You can be trained to run a machine, but you must be educated if you want to successfully run your life. Training usually deals with practical facts, while education deals with timeless truths and principles. The trained man has mastered methods; the educated man understands why those methods work. Training acquaints you with the science of your calling, education with the art.

Those two aspects of life are not contradictory; they are complimentary. Unfortunately, on some campuses, they are competitive, as the "practical" departments and the "pure academic" departments fight it out for attention and support. It is a futile and unnecessary war, because we need both.

To be sure, the effective minister needs to master certain skills, and he would not need to go to school to learn them. He could apprentice himself to some pastor and over the years discover and develop his abilities to study, prepare messages, make visits, win souls, baptize, serve the Lord's Supper, and so on. However, ministry involves *the whole man*; and it is a tragedy when a ministry is out of balance. Pity the pastor who is valuable only for what he *does,* not for what he *is.* Effective training can help a man get the job done, but solid education can put some depth and substance into that work.

Most younger ministers in their first charges complain because the school did not adquately train them for the practical demands of the ministry: how to run meetings, how to deal with stubborn members, how to plan a church program that will work, how to get rid of incompetent Sunday School teachers, and so on. The list could be endless because the demands are endless. But it is impossible for the practical theology instructor to solve every problem and tell you how to accomplish every task. He will share principles and methods from his own experience and study, but he certainly will not attempt to give you a complete kit of tools. There are some things you will have to learn on the job.

But don't miss the point: the kind of job you do with those tools will pretty much depend on *the kind of person you are,* and that is where your total education comes in. Training can hand you a bow and arrow and teach you how to shoot, but only education can direct you to the right target and help you hit it. It takes a good man to do a good job with good tools, and one of the purposes of education is the making of a good man.

Something else is true: training equips you to do things that, to some extent, can be measured; but education produces long-range dividends that cannot be measured or evaluated right now. Education is a part of that total development of life that is essential to long-term success, not just immediate "results." Charles Spurgeon may not have graduated from college and seminary, but he was a devoted student and a voracious reader. He was a self-educated man, and he read more than commentaries on the Bible!

We say all of this just to encourage you not to substitute education for training or training for education, because you need both. However, don't belittle your education because you think it robbed you of training. Education enables you to grow in both your training and your living; without education, you are at a standstill. Ministers, like doctors and brokers, can always attend another seminar to upgrade and update their professional skills. But the time to get the basic education that will prepare you for life is now. That is not to imply that graduation means your education is completed! A truly educated man knows how much there is to learn. But it does mean that you have that stable foundation on which you can build for the rest of your life.

If your campus experience is to be an enriching one, you must be sure you are called of God to be a minister of the Word. This is not to say that you have all the details worked out; it does mean that you belong to Him, that you are available for whatever He has planned for you. There will be further steps of dedication and devotion, to be sure; but all of them will depend on that glorious step of surrender when God called you to become His servant. No strings attached, no escape clauses in the contract, no conditions demanded—just a total giving of yourself to God to do His will. The double-minded student will be unstable in all his ways, to paraphrase James 1:8. Preparation for ministry is not an easy thing. You will need the strength of this kind of commitment to help carry you through.

It doesn't take long for the bright-eyed student to discover that a Christian school is not the gateway to glory. A campus family, like any family, has its share of problem people and difficult situations, possibly more. You are paying to be there, so finances play a part. You are there to learn, so there must be such things as instructors, books, lectures, and tests. Oh, yes,

there are also grades. You also have the abundance of inter-
personal relationships that must develop when several hundred
people live and study together. We expect more from Christians,
of course, but we don't always get it. But, to be honest, let's
confess that you and I don't always *give* our best; so *we* might
also be a part of the problem. Your Greek professor wants to be
your friend and assist you with your personal needs, but first of
all, he must teach you Greek. The fact that he prays with you
privately doesn't mean he has to give you an *A* in the course. He
may, in fact, fail you.

So, one of the first principles you must learn is that your
spiritual life and academic life must go together. No amount of
dedication can compensate for bad study habits or poor grades.
If dedication means anything at all, it means doing our best for
the Lord. Beware of that subtle dichotomy that can creep into
your life and separate things "spiritual" from things "scholas-
tic." What God has joined together, we must not put asunder.

There was once a seminary student who was always "getting"
new sermon outlines from the Lord. Right in the middle of his
Greek studies, he would shout to his wife, "The Lord just gave
me another outline!" However, when grades came out, he didn't
do so well in his Greek class; which encouraged his wife to
remark, "How strange that the Lord gives you all those outlines,
but He never seems to give you any Greek."

You must guard yourself against another danger, that of getting accustomed to your blessings. On a Christian campus, it is
very easy to take your blessings for granted and even start to
disparage them. Heed the words of George MacDonald: "Nothing is so deadening to the divine as an habitual dealing with the
outside of holy things." Read that statement again and ponder
it.

Take, for instance, your attitude toward the Bible. In many of
your classes, the Bible will be a textbook, and, occasionally, it
will be treated critically. That is especially true in your exegesis
classes. If you are not careful, your constant use of the Bible
may rob it of that special distinction that the Word of God
always deserves. It is not that we alter the Bible, but that our
own hearts get hard. The constant use of the Bible for "proof
texts" might create an attitude in you that is almost anti-Bible!
One Bible school student became so disgusted with the "proof
text" approach that he stopped using his Bible for his personal

devotions, because all he was seeing were proof texts! Fortunately, he outgrew that and took 1 Thessalonians 2:13 seriously: "And for this reason we also constantly thank God that when you received from us the word of God's message, you accepted it not as the word of men, but for what it really is, the word of God, which also performs its work in you who believe."

Your daily devotional time is not an opportunity to catch up on your Bible reading for Bible survey classes. Nor is it a time to search for sermon outlines for senior preaching. It is a time for God to speak to you personally out of His Word, because without Him, you can accomplish nothing. A satisfying devotional time is the foundation for a successful Christian life and ministry. This doesn't mean you must imitate Martin Luther and spend three hours a day in prayer. Your devotional experience must be tailored to your needs and your personality. You and God can work it out if you will permit Him. Try to meet Him daily; but, if for some reason you miss a day, don't go on a guilt trip and walk the aisle at the next invitation. It's when the neglect of your prayer time becomes an agreeable habit that you are in trouble. Don't let it go that long.

Not only can the Word of God and prayer become commonplace to you, but so can the public worship of God. You may not believe this, but chapel is as much a part of your ministerial training as your classroom assignments. Just make up your mind that regular chapel attendance will be a scheduled part of your day or week, and stop arguing about it. Never use chapel to catch up on either your reading or your sleeping. Use the time to worship God. The speaker may not always capture your undivided attention or evoke your unsolicited praise, but give him a hearing just the same. Nowhere on campus does the golden rule need practicing more than during services in chapel. If you attend a school where the dean requires you to sign in for chapel, don't permit that minor regulation to rob you of the values gained. Get used to it.

The academic community is not a local church, but as the people of God, they must meet for corporate worship. You never can tell when God has some special word for you. To be sure, we have sometimes gone to chapel needing bread and have received stones; but we have also gone to chapel and been enriched in wonderful ways. More than one servant of God can mark a turning point in his life because of a chapel message. So take chapel seriously. Other students may criticize it and ignore it, but don't follow their example. Prepare yourself for chapel as you would for a church service. Keep your heart and mind open to God's truth, and He will bless you. One day, when you are out on the field in ministry, things you have heard in chapel will come back to you with new force; so, if you want the dividends then, you had better make the investments now.

One of the chief indoor sports of ministerial students is criticizing chapel speakers. That is one activity you will want to shun, especially after you have had some courses in homiletics and hermeneutics. The chapel speaker may not slice the bread exactly the way the textbook explains, but you can still feed your soul on it. Your adversary enjoys it when you start to dissect a sermon, because then you are acting as a judge and not as a needy listener. Even a rose loses its beauty if you take it apart. Don't get into the habit of performing autopsies on every chapel service. One of these days, *you* will be the preacher, and your judgment will come back to you.

You also need a guard against jesting about spiritual things. Each profession has its "official humor" which is really innocent if the motive is sincere. Wit and humor are one thing; derisive jesting is quite something else. What Phillips Brooks called "the clerical jester" can cheapen that which really is very precious. There is humor in the Bible, but the Bible is not a joke book. There is humor in everyday life, and we pity the person whose solemnity or piety is so great that he cannot see the funny side of life. There is a humor that refreshes, and there is a humor that destroys. Joking about spiritual matters will only rob you of the glory and excitement that those things could convey to you.

Personal relationships are important at school. If you wish, you may become a holy hermit and ignore the society of your fellow students; but if you do, you will improverish yourself. It is likely that God will give you some lifelong friends during your campus years; in fact, He might even give you a lifelong mate! (That's not why you are in school, but it could be a blessed fringe benefit.) No student can stay glued to the books; it's as bad for his health as it is for his education. Leisure time is not lost time; it is time invested. The archer and the violinist both unstring their bow. Physical recreation, even a walk around the campus, is good for both the body and the mind. Don't feel that you have to *earn* free time. Schedule it and guard it as religiously as you do your prayer time.

You will not like everybody on your campus, and not everybody will like you. (That's fair, isn't it?) Most Christian campuses have just about the same kinds of students. You will find the superpious crowd with haloes so tight they get headaches. Often they *give* headaches to everybody else, but you'll have to accept them and love them. Just don't be infected by them. Every Christian campus has its share of holy headhunters, students who stalk about looking for heresy and carnality. They question every statement a professor makes, they investigate what translations of the Bible are being used, and they generally make big nuisances of themselves. Again, learn to accept them and love them. Some of them are lonely and that is their way of escape; or they are insecure and they find peace in making war together. Some of them just need to grow up.

You may also have a band of zealots, people who measure spirituality by the number of tracts you've given out, or the number of converts you can report. They aren't always concerned about their grades, but they are always willing to give a testimony in chapel to tell what God has done through them. Certainly you ought to be a faithful witness and touch as many lives as you can for Christ, but don't let the statisticians intimidate you. If you have been called of God to go to school, *then being a student is your ministry for Him.* When our Lord returns, He will judge you on the basis of what He gave *you* to do; and if preparation for ministry is His calling, then you had better be found faithful (Luke 12:41-48). Scholarship is stewardship, and we had better be found faithful stewards.

Every campus has its rules, and it is our guess that you knew what they were before you arrived at school. Some schools are more rigid than others, and no set of rules can guarantee obedience. In fact, with some people, the very presence of rules is an invitation to disobedience. You will see living examples of Romans 7 on every Christian campus. We would advise you not to try to change the rules. It has been our experience that it is not the rules themselves that create problems, but the way the administration interprets and applies them. The dean's office may not win the consistency award, but that is not your problem. Hundreds, perhaps thousands, of other students managed to get an education at your school in spite of the rules, and no doubt you can succeed as well.

There will probably be a small band of "joy boys" on campus, religious Robin Hoods whose life-style (a word that can excuse a multitude of sins) challenges the rule book and keeps the dorm advisors on their toes—and their knees. The poor we always have with us, so merely accept them as a part of the fixtures and don't imitate their example. Some of them will eventually mature and become useful servants of God. It would be embarrassing to list here the names of some preachers we know who, when they were in school, would have been thrown out bodily were it not for the patient love of a praying dean. Let him that readeth understand.

You will not like everybody on campus, but you can still show them Christian love. Love, after all, is an act of the will. It means treating others the way God treats us, and the way we want others to treat us. We cannot always command our affections, but we can control our emotions and actions. Some of the "problem people" on campus are actually needy people whose attitudes and antics are disguises, protective coloration that keeps you from seeing the real person. A friendly smile, a personal greeting, a listening ear, even a time of conversation and prayer, could make a difference in both of your lives. God can teach us many lessons from people we don't agree with, so be open to His leading.

Everybody in your campus community can teach you something, and you have your contribution to make to them. We can learn from our equals as well as our masters. Even a casual contact can lead to lasting enrichment. "A single conversation across the table with a wise man," said Longfellow, "is better than ten years' more study of books." The book of human nature can teach you much, and it is important that the minister of the Word know how to read and understand that book. In fact, the people you meet on campus you will meet during the rest of your life, so get to know them. You will discover them in your first congregation and in your last; their names and faces will change, but the people themselves will stay pretty much the same. Read their lives, not to condemn, but to learn. Get to know people; you will be working with them for the rest of your life.

Just a word about your relationship to the faculty and administration of the school. They are people just like anybody else. This means that they make mistakes and sometimes create problems. They have their joys and sorrows, their good days and

Sometimes you may learn more from your peers
than from the professors.

bad days, and appreciate being appreciated. They can't perform miracles; if they could, they probably wouldn't be where they are. Accept them as human beings with feelings, as fellow Christians under God's authority, as servants of God who must one day give an account of their ministry. Try to remember that you are under their authority *to learn from them,* not to argue with them or try to impress them with how much you think you know. Most instructors are approachable, so take your problems or disagreements to them personally and privately. Don't use class time for personal matters; you have no right to rob the other students of their education.

We suggest that you pray for your instructors by name in your private devotions. Remember the administration as well. It's amazing how much easier it is to get alone with somebody you sincerely pray for on a regular basis. Keep in mind that most school personnel have families to care for. Every late paper or examination may be added work for them at a time when they would enjoy doing something else. Asking for special times of assistance can be a bit annoying, although most instructors are willing to go the extra mile to help you. Just remember that they are human and they have lives to lead.

Maintain an attitude of respectful openness. Feel free to discuss academic or spiritual problems with your teachers, but beware of airing private opinions and prejudices. As difficult as it may be, try to separate the *contents* of the course from the instructor's *style* of delivery. The professor who bores you may excite the person next to you. Each teacher has his or her own approach to teaching, and some are better than others. It is not likely that you or the school president is going to change any of them, so learn to adapt and stop complaining. It is our experience that we learn faster and learn more if we approach each class with a positive attitude toward the instructor.

One seminary student we know took a theology course under an internationally known scholar, and during the first few lectures the student was disappointed and almost turned off. But he determined to get as much out of the course as possible; after all, he did pay for it. That determination changed the entire situation, and in later months, what he learned in that class greatly enriched his preaching. Don't expect every teacher to fit the mold you have made for him. The instructors who don't fit that mold may end up teaching us the most.

You will probably be assigned to a faculty advisor. Get to

know him and let him assist you. If for some reason the two of you don't "click" immediately, give yourself time. Pray about it and work at building bridges and not walls. Providence may have assigned you to the very advisor you need, but you haven't yet discovered why.

Often a student will feel drawn to a faculty member and a life-long friendship will develop. Such relationships are a joy to any teacher as he sees "his children" grow in grace and develop in the ministry. One of the few compensations of teaching is the knowledge that you are reproducing yourself in the lives of others as they minister around the world. Should you be granted such a friendship, cherish it, enjoy it, *but don't exploit it.* There is a fine line between "faculty friend" and "teacher's pet." Never use a faculty friend to get special privileges.

Grades (unfortunately) are a part of education. Sometimes they are accurate, and sometimes they are dead wrong. Most instructors try to give their students the benefit of the doubt, but occasionally they are in error and appreciate being told. You certainly have the right to discuss your grades with your teachers, and it might be enlightening to get their viewpoint. Sometimes grading is a rather subjective thing, and no two people will evaluate a term paper or a sermon outline in the same way. However, over the years, most teachers have developed a "sixth sense" when it comes to these matters, and their grades are not usually that far off. Unless you have had to do it yourself, you have no idea how difficult it is to read and grade class material week after week, year after year.

Some instructors have an area of expertise apart from their chosen subject. One may collect rare Bibles; another may be an expert on Bible coins; still another may be an expert on some era of church history. Fortunately, most professors are more than happy to share their hobbies with interested students, so make use of this tuition-free education. However, don't use such an experience as a means to "get next to the professor" and perhaps wheedle a better grade. And don't make a pest out of yourself!

What about students who "lose their faith" during their years of preparation? Well, that does happen, occasionally, and for different reasons. Some students had little or no faith to begin with. They were propped up by some religious idea, and when the props were knocked down, the students fell. One purpose of education is to expose you to different views of various subjects, and some people's "faith" can't survive that kind of exposure. If you challenge their favorite theory or view of prophecy, they may feel threatened. Well, the sooner you get rid of man-made scaffolding and start building your faith on a solid foundation, the better off you will be. Even the Lord shakes things so that the things unshakable will remain (Hebrews 12:25-29).

A faith that can't be tested can't be trusted. All truth comes from God; so, if your faith is in Christ and His Word, your educational experience ought to strengthen your faith, not destroy it. You never need to fear the truth. Men's theories need not upset you, but truth could very well disturb you; *and that is good.* You may find out that what you thought was a theological doctrine is really only a religious tradition. Your pastor at home may have shared as "Bible truth" that which is only the ideas of men. Don't be too hard on your pastor; just accept truth as God gives it to you, and let it make a difference in your life. During the course of your life, you will reexamine and rearrange the furniture of your faith, but the foundation will never change.

If anything, a real education helps us to be more tolerant of those who differ with us. Tolerance is not compromise; it is courtesy. It is simply giving to the other person the same privilege of honest enquiry that we want him to give to us. It's difficult to improve on Augustine's counsel: "In essentials, unity; in nonessentials, liberty; in all things, charity."

Sometimes this matter of "losing your faith" is not an intellectual problem so much as a moral and spiritual problem. Christian students preparing for ministry can sin just as easily as anyone else, and sin always erodes a person's faith. If you neglect the cultivation of your spiritual life, talk a great deal about "freedom," and live just to please yourself, then you might one day have a crisis of faith. It is easier to live for Christ on a secular campus, where the enemy is watching, than on a Christian campus, where a facade of respectability (and perhaps hypocrisy) shields us. ("If you won't tell on me, I won't tell on you.")

Perhaps the cause of failure might be a bad relationship with a fellow student or an instructor. You know the argument: "If *he's* a Christian, then I want nothing to do with Christianity!" Well, that is a good excuse, but a poor reason, for abandoning ship and wrecking your faith. It takes a diamond to cut a diamond. You and your friends will accept rude behavior from unsaved people and say, "Well, they don't know the Lord." But when *Christians* give us a hard time, we take it out on the Lord and the school! All of us have to roll with the punches, even if the boxer is wearing evangelical gloves. To blame someone else for our failure may ease our own conscience, but it still doesn't make the failure right.

You will have to face and try to solve many tough questions during your educational career, in fact, during your lifetime, and some of them you may never really answer. The stark realities of church history, the human fallacies revealed by philosophy, the unanswered problems of theology, can either be stepping-stones or stumbling blocks for you, depending on your own integrity and your willingness to let God know more than you do. The worst thing you can do is pretend that these problems don't exist. The next worst thing is to accept simplistic answers from a pamphlet mailed out by some media preacher who probably doesn't know what the real questions are.

It comes as a shock to some students that the right kind of education raises questions as well as answers them. Your professors are not professional "answer men" like the newspaper columnists. They are guides on the pathway of truth. They want to teach you how to face truth honestly, think for yourself, dig into the Word of God for direction, and come to decisions that will make a practical difference in your life. There are some things we are *always* sure of, because God has made those things clear in His Word. There are other matters that must always exercise our minds and test our faith, because good and godly men have wrestled with them for centuries. However, the mature person builds his life on the certainties (and we have plenty of them!) and exercises his spiritual muscles on the questions. Dr. John Hutton said, "A man who gives up his Christianity only surrenders a life of faith troubled by doubt, for a life of doubt troubled by faith."

Some of the greatest servants of God have had temporary eclipses of faith. Fortunately, an eclipse doesn't extinguish the sun or moon; it just blots out the light for a short time. Sometimes personal problems trigger the crisis; sometimes it is an attack from the adversary. Your best response is to admit it, talk it over with a trusted and mature friend, continue your personal devotional life at whatever level you can, and give God time to bring you through. There is a difference between doubt and deliberate unbelief, between questioning God's ways and denying God. The patriarchs and prophets had their hours of darkness, and so might we; but we must never doubt in the darkness what God teaches us in the light. There is no need to abandon ship simply because the storm is blowing and you are not sure how the compass works. God has proved Himself faithful to you in the past, and He will not forsake you now.

Well, we end up where we started: preparation for ministry is the making of the man. Whatever builds you up spiritually, intellectually, morally, physically, will help make you the minister God wants you to be. Whatever challenges you and calls forth your best efforts will add to your strength and stature. You can drift through school and possibly graduate and "make it," or you can determine to give it your best and get out of your experience all that God wants you to have. It would be a tragedy to waste all your time and money and energy!

We began with a quotation from Phillips Brooks, so we shall close this chapter with another quotation. (By now, you've discovered that we're partial to Brooks.) Here it is: "Do not pray for easy lives. Pray to be stronger men and women. Do not pray for tasks equal to your powers. Pray for powers equal to your tasks."

That's good enough to write in the front of your Bible!

I have no objections to churches so long as they do not interfere with God's work.

Brooks Atkinson

Jesus, yes! The church, no!

Hippie slogan of the 1960s

O be not too quick to bury the church before she is dead!

John Flavel

It is of no avail to talk of the church in general, the church in the abstract, unless the concrete particular local church which the people attend can become a center of light and leading, of inspiration and guidance, for its specific community.

Rufus Jones

I love Thy Church, O God!
Her walls before Thee stand,
Dear as the apple of Thine eye,
And graven on Thy hand!

Timothy Dwight

Christ also loved the church and gave Himself up for her.

Ephesians 5:25

I do my share on behalf of His body (which is the church).

Colossians 1:24

Shepherd the flock of God among you, exercising oversight, not under compulsion, but voluntarily, according to the will of God; and not for sordid gain, but with eagerness.

1 Peter 5:2

6

Something About the Church

This thing that we call "ministry" is closely related to another rather elusive thing that we call "the church." The way you look at the church will help to determine how you prepare for ministry and then how you carry out that ministry on the field. It will also help to determine how you measure your ministry; so it helps to know what the church is and what it is supposed to do.

But therein lies the problem: even the best scholars and preachers we know, and the best books we read, simply do not agree. There are so many images of the church in the New Testament that it is difficult to achieve a balanced view and maintain a balanced ministry.

There are those who see the church as *an army,* and they develop a rather militant view of the ministry. Interestingly enough, this militancy reveals itself in two opposite extremes. The conservative militants fight against "the world" and adopt a separatist posture, while the more liberal militants seek to change the world and get involved in activities like protest marches, sit-ins, lobbying, and so on. That the same metaphor (the army) should produce such opposite ministries is proof that the minister brings to his study of the church a certain number of theological presuppositions. A metaphor is as much a mirror as a window.

In recent years there has been an emphasis on the church as *a body.* It has been popular to have "body-life" groups even within old-line traditional churches. For a time, the body-life movement was almost a cult, with people going around asking one another, "And what is *your* gift, my brother?" until we all needed the gift of patience. For the most part, pastors involved in body-life ministry look upon themselves as "pastor-teachers," and Ephesians 4 as their declaration of independence.

65

The image of *the harvest* is also popular, especially among ministers who want to build "superaggressive churches" that bring in the sheaves. Some of them have their own style of evangelism and look with suspicion on people who might take a different approach. The pastor is in charge of the harvest, assisted by a staff of specialists and supported by the church members. Most of his preaching is geared to reaping the whitened fields.

Along with the harvest metaphor is that of *fishing,* both of which are certainly biblical. The church exists primarily to equip fishermen and fisherwomen to drop the hook and throw out the nets for a catch. Oddly enough, the recurring phrase heard among these people is not "fishing" but "soul-winning," an image taken from hunting, not fishing. (Proverbs 11:30 is the key text: "The fruit of the righteous is a tree of life; and he that winneth souls is wise." The Hebrew word translated "winneth" in KJV* simply means "to take, to seize, to acquire." It can even mean "to take a wife." But the image seems to be that of a hunter after his prey.)

Some of the more mystical ministers like to see the church as *a bride.* Their messages emphasize communion with God and separation (perhaps isolation) from the world. Phrases like "the deeper life" and "the victorious life" are important in their vocabulary. These people certainly rejoice when a sinner turns to Christ, but that is not the main thrust of their ministry. The church is an exclusive "in group" that puts spiritual fellowship ahead of everything else. Any other activities are merely a by-product of that fellowship.

Those who see the church as a *family* or a *fellowship* major on doing things together with a niche for everybody. Christian photographers can get together and discuss how their spiritual lives are developing. Believers interested in the American Civil War can talk over old times. There is probably a group for seamstresses, antique collectors, Tolkein fans, and ventriloquists, because the church is made for fellowship. The pastor often becomes sort of a ringmaster at a three-ring circus, but things are exciting and new horizons of fellowship are constantly opening up. Church organization is rather fluid, public meetings are on the informal side, the minister is "just one of the boys," and a good time is had by all.

---

* King James Version.

What the pastor sees when he looks at his congregation
will pretty much determine how he relates to the church.

We could go on, but it would be boring and unnecessary. There are dozens of images of the church in the New Testament, and each image carries its own special message and emphasis. Now you can understand better why Christians don't always agree on what the church is and how it is supposed to function. Metaphors are important because they help us get our hands on abstract truth; but when you isolate one image, and make it the only image, then you start to create problems. We believe that every local assembly needs different images *at different times.* There are times when the "harvest" image is important; at other times, the "family" or the "body" might be what is needed. Those images are complementary, not contradictory. The wise minister must know his church and know which image best describes it as well as which image is most needed.

The problem is, many of the *members* of the local assembly don't really know what the church is or what the church is supposed to do. That makes it difficult for them to know what their minister is supposed to do, so you end up with as many job descriptions as there are members. Mrs. Jones wants her pastor to be a deep devotional speaker, while Mrs. Howard (who once belonged to a "soul-winning church") expects each sermon to be boldly evangelistic. The college students in the congregation keep listening for incisive social criticism and a call for militant action. So the sheep get lost in the harvest field, while the fish slip through the nets and the soldiers wait for someone to call them to battle. If there is anything worse than a mixed metaphor, it's a confused ministry.

The important thing to remember is that you are preparing to minister to *individuals,* not to a group. It is a dangerous thing to believe the myth that *the church* gets things done in the world. It is *individuals* who get things done in and through the church—and sometimes, in spite of the church! The gospel is preached to individuals, and it is through individuals that the Spirit of God must work.

Of course, those individuals desperately need each other because they belong to each other and minister to each other. That includes the pastor. You will learn a great deal from your people, and the more you learn from them, the better you will be able to teach them. The ideal is that all of you "may be mutually encouraged by each other's faith" (Romans 1:12, NIV).*

New International Version.

So if at this stage in your life the concept of the church is not too clear, don't despair. Keep learning, keep growing, and keep ministering to people in love, and things will get brighter. Sometimes your people will be like sheep needing a patient shepherd; at other times, they will be soldiers who need a courageous commander. The wise pastor must be like the men of Issachar, "who understood the times, with knowledge of what Israel should do" (1 Chronicles 12:32). That requires spiritual discernment, and God will give it to you as you grow in your experience and knowledge. Don't focus on only one image of the church; it will probably put your life and ministry out of balance.

For that reason, don't get excited about every new scheme for church growth or church renewal. What does this concept mean to the individuals in my church? is the key question. You are not ministering to an abstract concept, or even to a group; you are ministering to individuals.

At the same time, we have to accept the fact that the church *is* an organization, a voluntary group of individuals who work together for the glory of God. Some of our "body-life" friends like to remind us that the church is really an *organism;* but we, in turn, remind them that if an organism isn't organized, it will die. Each of the images of the church emphasizes some kind of order: the sheep follow a shepherd; the stones must be in proper place in the temple; the bride must be properly adorned for her bridegroom; the priests have their special places in their service; and so on. The human body is the most wonderfully organized organism in the world. No wonder Paul used it to picture the church.

The warning that our "body-life" friends are issuing is a valid one: don't let the organization kill the organism. It's the old fable of the ant and the centipede. The ant asked, "How do you know which leg to move next?" The centipede replied, "I've never thought about that!" and the more he considered the question, the more paralyzed he became, until he was afraid to move at all! When any group starts emphasizing the *means* and not the *end,* it starts living for itself and not for the purpose for which it was started. To use the technical term, it has become institutionalized. When that occurs, the members start spending time, money, and energy just keeping the machinery going, and nobody asks whether anything is really being accomplished.

There is really no conflict between the *church organic* and the *church organized,* because the first supplies the dynamic for ministry and the second the direction. The organization must serve the organism; the church bylaws were made for man, not man for the bylaws. G. Campbell Morgan's philosophy of the local church program was a wise one: "A minimum of organization for a maximum of work." Try it!

When the ministerial student or younger minister looks at the organization of the average local church, he wonders how he will be able to manage. There are all kinds of books available on how to plan the church year, how to work with committees, and how to build a Sunday school for fun and profit; and you ought to read them and use what you can from them. But just keep in mind that *you are always a minister,* whether standing in the pulpit or sitting on the church board. You will learn a great deal about your people in committee meetings and church business meetings, and they will learn a great deal about you. Those meetings will give you many opportunities for quiet pastoral work, so don't complain that administration is taking you away from more important duties. If you take a negative attitude toward organizational ministry, you will only hurt yourself and the church. Again, focus on the individual, and use those administrative tasks as opportunities to be a better pastor.

"A ministry of growing power," said James Stalker, "must be one of growing experience." It is difficult for the church to rise above its leadership. The pastor must lead the way, and that means maturing in spiritual power, in wisdom, in pastoral skills, and in Christian character. Sometimes God will send you special trials just to help you grow. After all, you can't have mountain-tops without also having valleys.

One special area of concern must be the use of your time. Time is a precious commodity to ministers and to students, and it is *now* that you must learn to invest it wisely. If you ever find yourself saying, "I'll be glad when I get out of school and have more time!" put your hand over your mouth and repent. You will *not* have more time when you graduate from school; there will still be only twenty-four hours in a day—*and you will still have to use those hours carefully.* Commencement will not create some great cosmic shock that will suddenly turn you into an efficiency expert. The way you use your time now is pretty much the way you will use it when you are pastoring a church, when nobody is making you punch a clock or meet a deadline. If you are today a poor planner, a procrastinator, an excuse-maker, then you will continue to wear those titles; but you will suffer more for wearing them. Trying to pastor a church without knowing how to discipline your time is an invitation to ulcers, tensions in marriage, growing frustration, and a nervous breakdown.

The key, of course, is *planning based on priorities.* Decide what is really important to you, in the will of God; and on the basis of those priorities, arrange your daily and weekly schedule. The test of a good plan is the amount of "margin" you have around your life; emotional "breathing space," so to speak. The smart planner doesn't set his life in concrete and operate by a stopwatch. He gets things done on time, but he maintains flexible margins so he can handle life's interruptions and emergencies.

The simple secret is to *work ahead.* It's amazing how more relaxed life can be when you are ahead of your work. Make use of those "odd moments" to get things done. Tackle the really tough assignments first and get them out of the way. Discipline yourself to get ahead in your reading while you're traveling (provided you aren't driving) or even relaxing during a holiday. We have even made use of summer vacations to get a head start on collateral reading. Slavery? Of course not! Instead of ruining the holiday, it helped to give us more holidays during school months. It gives you a good feeling to know that *you* are controlling your schedule, and that you are not the victim of changing circumstances. Once we get behind, everything starts to fall apart. Let him who has ears to hear, hear what we say.

The principles that apply to time also apply to money: you can waste it or invest it. Jesus made it very clear that there is a close relationship between what you do with your money and how you handle the riches of God's Word. "He who is faithful in a very little thing is faithful also in much; and he who is unrighteous in a very little thing is unrighteous also in much. If therefore you have not been faithful in the use of unrighteous mammon, who will entrust the true riches to you?" (Luke 16:10-11). Alas, more than one servant of God has been careless in this area and has forfeited his testimony and his ministry.

What we said about time, we say about money: don't get the idea that you will handle it better when more is available. If you waste a small salary now, you will waste a larger salary later on.

It is important that *now* you get a handle on both your time and your money. You will not only be saving yourself present problems, but you will be avoiding worse problems in the future. Perhaps some expert on campus can help you with your money management.

If there is one phrase that best summarizes what the ministry of the church is all about, that phrase is *reconciliation based on compassion.* The church should be a compassionate community of believing people who love each other, and love a lost world, because they have personally been reconciled to God through faith in Jesus Christ.

But we live today in a broken world. If Shakespeare's Hamlet thought the times were "out of joint" in his day, he should see the world today! Sinners are destroying themselves and their world because they need to be reconciled to God. Even the believers need to be reconciled to each other! Homes need to be mended, broken friendships need to be repaired and strengthened, and churches need to be united in the ministry of reconciliation. If ever you get a bit foggy on what your commission is, read 2 Corinthians 5:18-21:

> Now all these things are from God, who reconciled us to Himself through Christ, and gave us the ministry of reconciliation, namely, that God was in Christ reconciling the world to Himself, not counting their trespasses against them, and He has committed to us the word of reconciliation. Therefore, we are ambassadors for Christ, as though God were entreating through us; we beg you on behalf of Christ, be reconciled to God. He made Him who knew no sin to be sin on our behalf, that we might become the righteousness of God in Him.

The devil is busy tearing things apart, but God is working in and through His church to put things back together again (Ephesians 1:9-12). There are many good things you can do with your life, but the greatest is the ministry of reconciliation. Let that be central in your studies and your service, and you will be ready for the church and the ministry God has called you to fulfill.

We suggest you read *I Believe in the Church,* by David Watson (Grand Rapids: Eerdmans, 1978). The author has an Anglican outlook but is balanced in the way he deals with church matters.

Divinity consists in use and practice, not in speculation and meditation. Every one that deals in speculations, either in household affairs or temporal government, without practice, is lost and nothing worth.

Martin Luther

Christianity knows no truth which is not the child of love and the parent of duty.

Phillips Brooks

If Christian ministers really believe it [Christian doctrine] is only an intellectual game for theologians and has no bearing upon human life, it is no wonder that their congregations are ignorant, bored, and bewildered.

Dorothy Sayers

Do not imagine that these great mysteries are completely and thoroughly known to any of us.

Maimonides

A clash of doctrines is not a disaster—it is an opportunity.
Alfred North Whitehead

I do not demand at all that people agree with me or my opinion or my say-so, except upon condition that they first recognize that what I teach is useful.

John Calvin

All true theology is thus intensely practical. That is why all theories purporting to show how the Gospel can be made relevant to man, even modern man, in his need, are by their very nature impossible, for they are substituting an intellectual relation for the practical relation which God himself has established in Jesus Christ.

T. F. Torrance

A system-grinder hates the truth.

Ralph Waldo Emerson

7

Meet the Queen

Theology is no longer considered the "queen of sciences," but in spite of that, don't dethrone her before you have opportunity to get better acquainted. The modern shallow attitude that croons, "Don't give us theology; we just want practical truth for the heart!" would never get to first base with the apostles and prophets, let alone the church Fathers and the Reformers. We need precision in theology as much as we need precision in medicine, money, and mechanics. Can you imagine a sick man saying to his doctor, "Doc, it makes no difference whether you remove my appendix or my liver, just so I know you are there." If devotional truth is not based on doctrinal truth, it is merely religious sentimentalism; and it will take more than a sentimental church to win a world for Christ.

It is a devastating truth that we become like the God that we worship (Psalm 115). What we believe about God helps to determine how we think, act, and relate to others. Of course, there are godly people who serve Christ faithfully and yet probably can't even spell "theology," but that is no argument for ignorance. We should love God with the mind as well as the heart and the strength. Churches need to get better acquainted with the God they profess to love and worship. It is significant and gratifying that a book like J. I. Packer's *Knowing God* should become so popular. Obviously, it meets a great need. Pity the congregation that must be addressed, "What therefore you worship in ignorance, this I proclaim to you" (Acts 17:23).

Nothing will stretch your mind or encourage your spiritual growth like a reverent study of theology. Note that we said *reverent*. God makes Himself known to the meek and lowly, those who want to learn more because they want to live better lives for God's glory. Theology is intensely personal and practical. It is not a subject for spinning beautiful webs, but for building useful lives. "Piety before theology," warned Henry Ward Beecher. "Right living will produce right thinking." Jesus said, "If any man is willing to do His will, he shall know of the teaching, whether it is of God" (John 7:17). Obedience is still the organ of spiritual knowledge.

Systematic theology, of course, begins with categories and therefore reflects the theologian's system of thought. In that sense, it is artificial; but so is the dictionary or a blueprint. If we are going to think about God, we must have some kind of order in our thinking; but we need to recognize the fact that our system is but a tiny expression of what God is. A college president was walking through the chemistry lab one day and paused to watch an experiment in action. He noted that the professor had made a mistake in writing the formula on the blackboard, but the experiment went on successfully just the same. Later, the professor corrected his mistake. Sometimes our feeble explanations and definitions are in error, but that will not change God. Faith can still relate to Him and love can still obey Him, and He will help us correct the formula in due time.

Your professors will tell you that systematic theology is "the science concerning God." The basis is honest exegesis in the Word of God, and the expression of it is a godlike life. But you will also be introduced to *biblical theology,* which deals with God's progressive revelation of Himself in the Bible. It is a necessary balance to systematic theology because biblical theology does not begin with preconceived categories of thought. It goes to the text and lets the text speak for itself. It sees the progressive unfolding of doctrine from age to age as recorded in Scripture. Biblical theology is important to accurate preaching of the Word, for it is easy for a preacher to read into the Old Testament narrative what is taught more clearly in the New Testament. "What *did* this mean to the original writer or speaker?" is a preliminary question to "What *does* this passage mean to the church today?"

In recent years, there has been a new interest in both *historical* theology and *natural* theology. The first traces the development of the understanding of doctrine throughout the history of the church, and shows how those doctrines influenced the life and ministry of the church. The second seeks to understand God from His creation, apart from the biblical revelation. Our Roman Catholic friends have majored in this approach over the years, but they don't have a corner on the market.

Of course, all of this must issue in practical theology, the out-working of divine truth in human life through the church. It is tragic when a school or a student divorces the various branches of theology from the practical meaning in the life of the believer and the church. H. H. Farmer, a leading British theologian, said in his "Yale Lectures" that he found it "increasingly hard to be interested in a theological discussion the bearing of which on the actual business of being a Christian in this tragic modern world—and the bearing of which, therefore, on the preacher's task of calling and helping men and women to be Christians in that world—I am not able to discern." Francis Bacon said it suc-cinctly: "Crafty men condemn studies; simple men admire them; and wise men use them."

The sane theologian always asks, "What does this doctrine mean to me personally? What does it mean to the people I am ministering to? What does it say about the world in which I am living and serving?" It is doubtful that many people attend church to hear the fine points of systematic theology; but they do want to know what God can mean to them in their everyday battles and burdens in life. He is the God of the living, not the dead, and that includes the "dead" theologians.

It is really an exciting thing to apply theology to life. Dorothy Sayers reminded us, "It is the neglect of dogma that makes for dullness. The Christian faith is the most exciting drama that ever staggered the imagination of man—and dogma is the drama." It is exciting to see how biblical doctrines relate to each other, how they center in Jesus Christ and at the cross, and how they magnify the grace of God. Doctrine gives us a solid foundation for life and ministry. Deeper insights into familiar doctrines are ever the mark of the growing Christian. Each doctrine is like a beautiful jewel with many facets, and the more we allow the light to shine through, the more beauty we see.

But there are dangers to avoid as you fill up your theology notebook, not the least of which is the tendency to file living truth into dead categories. Just as a loving husband and wife grow in their knowledge of one another and therefore enter into an ever-deepening relationship, so the student of theology must grow in his relationship with God as he gets to know Him better. The statistics on a driver's license are not the person who is described. Theological definitions and discussons are not God. The recipe is not the meal. The student must, by faith, accept all that God is and govern his life accordingly. Humility is one evidence of this deepening relationship. A tendency to argue and to debate minor matters is an evidence that this relationship is not deepening. A theologian needs a warm heart as well as a clear head.

Another danger is the attitude that one truth is the whole truth. All truth comes from God, and all truth intersects. One truth balances another truth, and a lack of balance in our own thinking can lead to heresy. Isolated doctrines can be very dangerous. "All err the more dangerously because each follows a truth," wrote Pascal. "Their mistake lies not in following a falsehood but in not following another truth." So one student majors on the gifts of the Spirit and sees all truth as it relates to that one area of revelation. Another emphasizes separation, or baptism, or even evangelism. Just as each member of the body needs the other members, so each doctrine needs the other doctrines. Try to avoid a narrow approach to truth, or what ought to be a busy highway will soon become a sterile, dead-end street.

Imagine a beautiful river as it runs through a lovely countryside. At certain points, the river divides into smaller rivers and creeks, forming islands here and there; and then it reunites to continue its journey. The people who live on those islands think that *their* river is the true river, while all other streams and creeks are suspect if not counterfeit. If all of the islanders could board a plane and fly *above* the countryside, they would see the true picture. That river is truth, and it is repeatedly dividing into smaller streams. Don't think that your little island is the whole world, or that your branch of the river is all the truth that exists. Go higher and higher and you will get the right perspective.

The young minister will soon discover that his theological training is eminently practical. To begin with, it gives him a solid footing for public and private ministry. Because God is what He is, we can know Him and introduce others to Him. As the pastor plans the worship service, he can focus the heart's attention on the God that he knows. In his own praying, privately and in the pulpit, he can talk to a God who is not a stranger. The seminarian who prayed, "Lord Jesus, you are our Father!" may have been asleep during the lectures on Christology.

But knowing God makes a pastor's counseling ministry much more effective. After all, the *counselor* doesn't solve the prob-

lems; it is *God* who must change people and redirect their lives.
A knowledge of counseling techniques and human psychology is
certainly necessary, if only to know what not to do. But a
knowledge of God, as He is revealed in the Bible, is even more
important. The two go together: we must understand man to
know how to introduce him to God. We must understand God
so we know how He relates to man's problems and needs. To be
able to affirm God's mercy and grace to a sinning person, to be
able to share God's love with a lonely person, to be able to relate
God's presence to a confused person, is what theology is all
about. And to be able to do so *without violating the personality
of the counselee* is also what theology is all about. Without
theology, counseling is merely religious persuasion, and
preaching is nothing but religious propaganda.

One seminarian reluctantly took a course on "The Atonement
in Scripture and History," and soon discovered that what he was
learning was helping him put a lot of other doctrinal material in
place. The centrality of the cross is important. It gives you
perspective when you discover how the church Fathers and the
Reformers struggled to understand and to defend the doctrine of
the atonement. It was said of Spurgeon that, no matter what his
text was, he ran as fast as he could across country to the cross.
We need more of that kind of preaching today.

At a time in history when so many adverse winds of doctrine
are blowing, it is good to have a solid doctrinal foundation
under your feet. The student who learns historical theology
discovers, of course, that Solomon was right—there is nothing
new under the sun. Every "new doctrine" that man manufac-
tures is only the stepchild of some ancient heresy. Historical
theology also helps you appreciate the men and women in
church history who studied, prayed, preached, wrote, and bat-
tled that the truth of the gospel might be preserved and preached
abroad. When you know what you believe, you are not easily
threatened by either religious heretics or religious hucksters.
Your convictions not only protect you, but they direct you. It is
even possible to get to know people you disagree with and to
learn from them! After all, it is the person of *conviction* who can
afford to relate to others, because he doesn't feel in danger. The
man who is unsure of himself will have a tendency to build walls
and not bridges. He will read only the "approved books" and go
to only the "approved meetings." He will get to know the "party line" better, but it is doubtful that the "party line" is as

enriching as the deep wells of theological truth found in the Word of God and the records of the church.

"One of the best things theology did for me," said one student, "was to help me be more precise in my thinking and my preaching. I found that I was using more discrimination in my use of words, including Bible words." No careful minister will settle for Sunday school definitions of Bible doctrines, such as, "Justification—just as if I'd never sinned." It is amazing how Christian people *want* doctrinal precision in the sermons that they hear. Some homileticians tell young preachers to avoid Bible language; but there is a technical vocabulary to the Christian life that simply cannot be avoided. Christians need to know the meaning of *justification, adoption, propitiation, grace, mercy,* and the other important Bible words. People in your congregation have worked hard to learn all sorts of technical language, from the mechanic in the garage to the scientist in the laboratory; and they appreciate an opportunity to stretch their minds on some solid biblical theology. Of course, we must make the words mean something in practical life; but the first step toward that is explaining what the words mean.

As you continue your study of theology, you may find yourself excited by one particular doctrine, and you may want to specialize. Fine, but don't divorce that doctrine from the rest of revelation. It is likely that a truly scholarly study of *one* doctrine will give you a better grasp of *all* doctrine, because God's truth is one. Only a bigoted religious huckster would preach one doctrine as though it were the whole of revelation. Your knowledge of sanctification, for example, would certainly increase your understanding of the nature of sin and the need for the ministry of the Holy Spirit. Properly studied, one vital doctrine can be a window that opens to wider vistas of truth that you perhaps would not otherwise see.

How do you continue your study of doctrine after you leave school?

For one thing, you get better acquainted with the books you have already read. It is amazing how a book that you once *had* to read suddenly becomes alive when you read it in the comfort of your home or at a cabin by a lake. Any book that is really worth reading once is worth reading twice. The context of pastoral work gives new meaning to old ideas. It might not be a bad idea to set up a reading program for old books. As you mature in your ministry, some of those texts will be set aside; but others will be worn out with use.

You will certainly want to keep up with the new books, but use discrimination. There are so many theological studies being published that even the experts can't keep up with them. Rely on the reviews in the better magazines. Phone your theology professor, or drop him a letter (with a stamped return envelope enclosed) and ask for a list of recent books that you ought to study.

Get acquainted with some good theologian and major on his works for a year or two. Augustine, Luther, Calvin, Strong, Warfield, Vos, Barth, Farmer, Torrance, and many others, are just waiting to teach you at your convenience. While you are at it, subscribe to a good publication that will help keep you abreast of what is going on in theological circles in the church. When a man becomes a lazy theologian, he becomes a lazy thinker, and that will make him a lazy preacher. Clear thinking and clear preaching always must go together.

Don't be afraid to discuss theology with your pastoral peers. That doesn't mean you have to turn every fishing trip or ball game into a seminar! Ministerial "small talk" can be as helpful and relaxing as a good nap; but there is also a time and place for "big talk." If you are near a theological campus, take time to visit the library, the bookstore, and the coffee shop, and take advantage of opportunities for special lectures or seminars. You will be tempted to attend all the "how-to-do-it" seminars, because practical training is a vital part of ministry; but don't forget the "*why*-we-do-it" meetings as well. There are some methods of ministry that are beneath the dignity of the truth of the gospel; but unless you know your theology, you will be trapped into using them, only to discover your mistake after the damage is done. The minister who says, "I don't care what your methods are just so long as your message is right!" had better meditate on 1 Thessalonians 2:1-6.

You will have to be a theologian all your life, either a good one or a bad one. Decide early in your school career that you are going to be a good one.

The immense value of church history and of the history of doctrine is the dimension of historical depth it gives to one's understanding of the faith, and the balance it brings to one's judgments. Did ever the church stand in greater need of this?

T. F. Torrance

Historic continuity with the past is not a duty, it is only a necessity.

Oliver Wendell Holmes, Jr.

It is not St. Augustine's nor St. Ambrose's works that will make so wise a divine as ecclesiastical history thoroughly read and observed.

Francis Bacon

One age cannot be completely understood if all the others are not understood. The song of history can only be sung as a whole.

Ortega Y. Gasset

God cannot alter the past, but historians can.

Samuel Butler

History is the discovering of the constant and universal principles of human nature.

David Hume

Civilization is a movement and not a condition, a voyage and not a harbor.

Arnold Toynbee

8

Catching Up with the Past

Emerson and Thoreau were chatting in Emerson's library, and the "Sage of Concord" remarked to his young friend that Harvard was now teaching all the branches of learning. "Yes," said Thoreau, "all of the branches, but none of the roots."

If our education doesn't help us get to the root of things, then it has not helped us a great deal. The educated person must think, ask questions, reflect on answers, and dare to dig deeper than current fads or popular opinions encourage. The educated person must be, in the original sense, a *radical*; for the word *radical* comes from a healthy Latin word that means "root." A true radical is one who gets to the root of a matter and tries to change things from the roots up. When he applied his ax to the roots of the trees, John the Baptist acted as a radical in the will of God.

But before you go after the roots, take some time to discover how they got there and what their purpose might be. That is where history comes in. It is unfortunate that some of our most gifted people in the church have been so busy changing the present that they haven't taken time to examine the past. Had they done so, they might have taken a different approach to ministry. Someone has said that most of the problems in this world are caused by people who haven't taken time to read the minutes of the previous meeting. The philosopher George Santayana expressed it well: "Those who cannot remember the past are condemned to fulfill it."

Most of us have endured dull history teachers and have mistakenly concluded that history itself is dull. When we hear the word *history,* we immediately think of lists of names and dates, maps and charts, and ponderous volumes by erudite scholars—the boring bric-a-brac of an embalmed academic pursuit. But history can be and ought to be exciting. The Christian in particular should be concerned about an understanding of history, since he believes that God is at work in the world, fulfilling His eternal purposes. Dr. A. T. Pierson used to say that "history is His story," and he was right.

So perhaps the first thing you must do is get rid of your adolescent prejudices against the study of history. More than one successful person has said that a knowledge of history is the best preparation for ministry, and we agree.

Why study history? After all, we are living in the present, getting people ready for the future; so why spend so much time and energy on the past? To begin with, a study of history gives you the best background for the study of all other subjects. Everything man studies and learns is a part of history. You don't write the history of a bee or a salmon; you write about the creature's *life cycle*. Insects and fish don't have histories, except in children's storybooks; they have life cycles, and what happens to one, happens to all. But each man and woman has his or her own history, because each one is unique. The tapestry of history is woven by kings and beggars, philosophers and charlatans, saints and sinners; and the better we know history, the better we can study anything that involves human life.

We have already said that a study of theology can help to give you perspective; but that is also true of history. Each age has its share of successes and failures, revolutions and reformations; and the better we know the past, the better we can understand the present. This does not mean that you must adopt a "cyclical view" of history to learn from history. It just means that, while the house of history is often remodeled, the inhabitants stay pretty much the same. "When I want to understand what is happening today," wrote Oliver Wendell Holmes, Jr., "or try to decide what will happen tomorrow, I look back." It pays to read the minutes of the previous meeting.

A study of history should give you an appreciation of the past. Modern man thinks he is superior to his father and grandfather, but he is not. Thoreau was right when he said that we had devised improved means to unimproved ends. Mankind made some fantastic strides forward long before our generation came on the scene, and we are the beneficiaries. If a study of history does not humble a person, he is reading through the wrong spectacles.

Since each age and each generation has its own special em-

In every school there is a group of joy-boys that you
will have to endure.

phasis, history helps us to conserve and rediscover the values of the past. One pastor we know made a study of the Greek Orthodox church and was amazed at the insights his study gave him into his own denomination's form of worship. Another student examined the "humanist movement" of the Reformation and the Age of Enlightenment, only to discover that what was passing for "humanism" today was a poor counterfeit. There are treasures in tradition if only we will dig them out.

When we understand history, we better understand ourselves. Knowing where we came from helps us understand where we are and, perhaps, where we are going. "I have always had one foot in the present and the other in the past," wrote historian Arnold Toynbee; and that is a good posture for a preacher. Without the past, we are a ship without a rudder, a tree without roots, a house built on the sand. When we study history, we are not ignoring the present; we are examining the present. "Life must be lived forwards," wrote Kierkegaard, "but can only be understood backwards." A healthy understanding of the past helps to provide a good corrective for the present. It also helps you to keep your thinking in balance.

Those who talk about "the dead past" have never really been there; for the past is not dead to the person who thinks. The popular historians, Will and Ariel Durant, said that they "buried [their] heads in the living past rather than the dying present." It is tragic that many Christians know better what has happened in the last week, thanks to the media, than what has happened in the last century. Not that we neglect the present! But of what value are the facts of the week as compared with the truths of the ages? We need both, and that is why we need history. History gives us not only the story of men and nations, but also the story of ideas and the varied things that make up culture. "Not to know what happened before one was born is to remain a child," wrote Cicero; which suggests that many people still have their minds in diapers. If nothing else, a study of history will expose a great deal of intellectual rubbish that passes for riches among people who don't know any better.

For the most part, history is people, so that Emerson was almost right when he wrote, "There is properly no history, only biography." He may have borrowed that sentiment from his friend Carlyle, who wrote: "The history of the world is but the biography of great men." History is a fascinating drama in which the characters remain the same but the settings get modernized. That explains why even the ancient historians may be read today with great profit: they are writing about people that we know and recognize. History can give us insight into character.

Sometimes a student becomes fascinated by a particular period in history, so he centers in on it and becomes a specialist. To his amazement, he discovers that that one limited period is a microcosm of all periods, including his own present time. Just as we urged you to specialize on one biblical doctrine, so we now urge you to become an expert on some important age in history. In fact, you might even combine the two. Again, you will see how all truth intersects and how the light from one lamp helps to ignite other lamps.

One student became interested in the life and ministry of John Wesley and his influence on the course of English history. At the same time, he investigated Wesley's doctrine of sanctification and the history of that doctrine from New Testament days to the present. That combined study gave him an "intellectual sun" around which the other academic planets could orbit with meaning and order, and he found himself "putting things together" in a practical way. Once you have been bitten by the "history bug," your symptoms may be the same.

In closing, we recommend that you read *How to Study History,* by Norman Cantor and Richard Schneider (Arlington Heights, Ill.: AHM, 1967). Another valuable book, and not too ponderous, is *Christianity and History,* by Herbert Butterfield (New York: Scribner's, 1950).

Any two philosophers can tell each other all they know in two hours.

Oliver Wendell Holmes, Jr.

Wonder is the feeling of a philosopher, and philosophy begins in wonder.

Plato

There is no defense, except stupidity, against the impact of a new idea.

P. W. Bridgman

The man who fears no truths has nothing to fear from lies.

Thomas Jefferson

God offers to every mind its choice between truth and repose. Take which you please—you can never have both.

Ralph Waldo Emerson

Peace if possible, but truth at any rate.

Martin Luther

Buy truth, and do not sell it.

Proverbs 23:23

See to it that no one takes you captive through philosophy and empty deception, according to the tradition of men, according to the elementary principles of the world, rather than according to Christ.

Colossians 2:8

It is necessary for a man to accept by faith not only things which are above reason, but also those which can be known by reason.

Thomas Aquinas

To be a philospher is not merely to have subtle thoughts; but so to love wisdom as to live according to its dictates.

Henry David Thoreau

9

A Passion to Connect

This chapter is about your study of philosophy, and the title comes from a statement by D. Elton Trueblood: "A philosopher is a person who, though his experiences may be varied and numerous, is not satisfied with their separateness, but has a passion to connect."

Of course, not everybody would define a philosopher in the same way. Our friend "Anonymous" says that a philosopher is "a blind man in a darkened room looking for a black cat that isn't there." (In all fairness, we should add that the philospher is supposed to have replied, "That's right, and if he were a theologian, *he would find it!*") That acid wit Ambrose Bierce defined philosophy as "a route of many roads leading from nowhere to nothing." But it required a certain amount of philosophical thought even to arrive at that definition.

Whether we like it or not, each of us is a philosopher of sorts, because each of us has an outlook on life based on convictions that we are fairly sure about. Aristotle defined philosophy simply as "the science which considers truth." Since all of us have to consider truth, according to Aristotle, all of us are philosophers. The Christian has a head start, of course, because he has found truth in Jesus Christ and His Word.

Formal philosophy deals with the basic questions of life. It does not only ask, "What is true?" but rather, "What is *truth?*" The philosopher wants to know why the "true" is true, why the "good" is good, and why the "beautiful" is beautiful. He is passionately interested in the essence of things, not the externals and the accidentals. Philosophy has to do with the nature of right thinking, and Christian philosophy has to do with the right living that ought to result from right thinking. The philosopher

The study of philosophy has a way of
keeping you humble.

doesn't just think; he also thinks about his thinking. He not only questions his answers, but he also questions his questions. In fact, framing the right questions is a vital part of true philosophical thinking.

Perhaps you have heard all your life that philosophy is the archenemy of Christian truth, and that people who start to dabble in philosophy end up losing their faith. True philosophy is not the archenemy of faith, because (as we have often said) all truth comes from God, no matter what the channel might be. Whether he likes it or not, every philosopher comes to his studies with certain presuppositions which he cannot prove. In other words, every philosopher starts with an act of faith: "I believe!" That is why we have atheistic and agnostic philosophers, as well as Christian philosophers.

As far as "losing your faith" is concerned, a quotation from Francis Bacon may calm your troubled spirit: "A little philosophy inclineth man's mind to atheism, but depth in philosophy bringeth men's minds about to religion." The experience of salvation does not lie at the end of a syllogism, but neither is the experience contrary to anything rational. William Temple, who was not only a profound thinker but also a devout believer, said in *Nature, Man and God*: "The heart of Religion is not an opinion about God, such as philosophy might reach as the conclusion of its argument; it is a personal relation with God."

Having said all of that, we must add that there is a certain kind of mind or attitude that can be threatened by the study of philosophy. Simply put, it is the mind that is afraid of truth. It is the mind that thinks on the basis of secondhand opinions or prejudices, and that will not examine its own thinking. That attitude is sometimes revealed in an attitude of arrogance, or an argumentative spirit. (Violence is often fear turned inside out.) Or, it may show itself in the opposite way by fleeing the field of battle, while hurling religious clichés at the enemy. If there is one thing we desperately need as we study philosophy, it is a feeling of true humility. "A good philosopher may be of any race or of any nationality," wrote D. Elton Trueblood; "he may be an atheist; he may be a scientist or a humanist; what he cannot be is *arrogant*. The necessary humility must not be the insincere humility of one who retreats from great problems, but the more genuine humility of one who tries to handle what he agrees is too big for him, and thus becomes a fool for philosophy's sake.''

The beginning philosophy student needs to beware of getting intoxicated by the arguments spun by those who would deny what we Christians believe. When you read their books, handle their material the way a scientist in the laboratory handles poison: he knows what is there, but he doesn't let it get into his system. That is what Paul had in mind when he wrote Colossians 2:8.

What relationship is there between philosophy and Christian ministry? Much of what we have already said about the study of history and theology would answer that question. Philosophy helps you to get perspective. It helps to teach you how to think and how to ask the right questions. It also exposes the intellectual rubbish that unfortunately passes for truth in too many places. We think that a proper study of philosophy adds to the glorious mystery of truth and life! "Philosophy begins in wonder," said Plato, and who are we to argue with him?

It is not likely that some aged saint, dying in the rest home, is going to ask you about existentialism; but you might confront this issue in a college-age Sunday school class or in personal counseling with a student home for the holiday. It will not be enough to throw proof texts at the questioner, because he is even questioning what "proof" the texts are. You must learn to think philosophically if you are going to meet the genuine needs of thinking people.

You also need to understand the mind-set of the society in which we live. To be sure, very few people could categorize their thinking as Hegelian, Aristotelian, existential, or Neo-platonic; but *you* had better be able to diagnose the case and know how to approach the patient and apply the remedy. *Encounter in the Non-Christian Era,* by John W. Sanderson, Jr. (Grand Rapids: Zondervan, 1970), is a good introduction to the kind of thinking going on in today's world; and, of course, the many books of Francis Schaeffer deal with this problem as well. Just keep in mind that the people you minister to are thinking a certain way and probably don't know all that is involved in their thinking. *You* must know, and that is where philosophy comes in. It can give you the weapons to fight with and the tools to build with.

We must hasten to add, however, that this does not mean that you approach the ministry of God's Word philosophically. People are not saved by believing a system or agreeing with an argument. They are saved through personal commitment to Jesus Christ. That is the argument Paul presents in 1 Corinthians 1:18—2:16, an argument every preacher of the Word ought to understand. It is not "the wisdom of this world" that changes people; it is the power of God at the cross. However, there is a proper "philosophy" of the Christian message that can be shared with those who are mature in the faith (see 2:6-16). In the pulpit, and in personal witness, you are not a philosopher; you are an ambassador.

Man is a thinking creature, and it is only right that he learn to think the highest thoughts in the most rational manner. The Christian is not looking *for* truth; he is looking *into* truth. "The fear of the LORD is the beginning of knowledge" (Proverbs 1:7). "The fear of the LORD is the beginning of wisdom" (Proverbs 9:10). Right thinking means loving God with the mind, just as right living means loving God with the heart and will.

A proper study of philosophy has a way of keeping you humble. You know how much you don't know. And when you do learn a truth, it humbles you even more. The more you penetrate into the nature of things (which is what philosophy is all about), the more inadequate you will feel, and the more you will depend on Christ, "in whom are hidden all the treasures of wisdom and knowledge" (Colossians 2:3).

As you progress in your studies of philosophy, you will begin to see how theology, philosophy, and history interact and intersect. The history of philosophy is not only a record of great minds grappling with great problems, but also of men and nations making decisions and suffering consequences. Ideas are not invisible abstractions; ideas have consequences. What people believe determines how people behave. You should better understand the lives of men and the histories of nations because of your familiarity with various philosophical systems.

A philosopher must cultivate a healthy distrust, but the Christian philosopher must never permit his questioning attitude to turn into doubt or unbelief. *Not* to ask questions is to remain ignorant. *Only* to ask questions is to grow in that ignorance. The Christian student of philosophy must maintain a healthy balance between question marks and exclamation points. Keep your goal in mind—the deeper understanding of God's truth so that you might enjoy a better life—and you are not likely to meander into skepticism. Major on the attitude described in Ephesians 4:15 and you will make it successfully—"but speaking the truth in love, we are to grow up in all aspects unto Him, who is the head, even Christ."

We suggest you read *All Truth is God's Truth*, by Arthur F. Holmes (Grand Rapids: Eerdmans, 1977).

Keep hard at the languages, for language is the sheath in which the sword of the Spirit rests.

Martin Luther

Who does not know another language, does not know his own.

Goethe

The drudgery of learning a foreign language sprinkled bitterness over all the sweetness of the Greek tales. I did not know a word of the language: and I was driven with threats and savage punishments to learn.

St. Augustine

I do not say that every preacher should become an expert in his knowledge of the New Testament Greek. That cannot be expected. I do not affirm that no preacher should be allowed to preach who does not possess some knowledge of the original New Testament. . . . But the chief reason why preachers do not get and do not keep up a fair and needful knowledge of the Greek New Testament is nothing less than carelessness, and even laziness in many cases.

A. T. Robertson

Indeed, it is often a lesson in moral philosophy to take a Hebrew dictionary and trace the gradual growth of meaning in certain words as their signification advances from things which are seen and temporal to those which are not seen and eternal. Persons who have made this a point of study can well sympathize with the saying of Luther, that he would not part with his knowledge of Hebrew for untold gold.

Canon Robert B. Girdlestone

As the title set over the head of Christ crucified, was the same in Hebrew, Greek, and Latin, so are the Scriptures the same, whether in the original, or other language into which they are faithfully translated. Yet, as the waters are most pure, and sweet in the fountain, so are all writings, Divine and human, in their original tongues.

John Robinson

10

"Tongues of the Learned"

One of the classic comments of seminary professors, passed down from generation to generation, is that their students "can't read Hebrew and Greek, and won't read English." The statement is an exaggeration, of course; otherwise no one would ever graduate. But it does point up the importance of Bible languages.

It should not be necessary to argue for the value of knowing how to use Hebrew and Greek. Tennyson once met a minister who confessed his ignorance of the original languages, and the poet exclaimed, "What! You the priest of a religion and cannot read your own sacred books!"

A working knowledge of the original languages is essential for good exegesis and Bible study, and those are the foundation for good preaching. That is not to say that a pastor must become a language scholar, but only that he appreciate the value of Hebrew and Greek and use the languages as tools for building his ministry. A minister is a slave to the commentators unless he can handle the languages. He must depend on books that are once removed from the text of Scripture. The most scholarly books are closed to him.

Of course, he will not parade his skills in public. We once endured a sermon by a minister who was doing graduate work in Hebrew, and it was obvious. His text (or pretext) was Psalm 103, but his exposition was a dull lesson in linguistics. We heard all about cognates and very little about the blessing of God. The man took a beautiful psalm and dissected it. We had come to church for a satisfying meal, but instead, we witnessed an autopsy. May his tribe decrease.

Every once in a while, a student shows up who just seems to have no aptitude for languages. Fortunately, they are a vanishing species, but you do occasionally meet one. What should he do with Hebrew and Greek? *The very best he can.* Even a passing exposure to the originals is better than nothing at all, for he will at least be able to use some of the "shortcut tools" that are now available. We are not pleading for everyone to imitate Alexander Maclaren, who did all of his sermon preparation from the original text. For that matter, we wouldn't qualify, ourselves. All we are asking is that you take the Bible languages seriously, realizing that they will be very valuable to you the longer you remain in the ministry.

We have met men who, on graduation from seminary, immediately sold all their language texts and tools, only to wish years later that they had kept them. The growing minister isn't satisfied with borrowing secondhand ideas from others; he gets to the place where he wants to mine his own gold. It is the working knowledge of Greek and Hebrew that puts the right tools into his hands. So please believe us when we say: the day will come when you will thank God for a working knowledge of the originals, so stay with the languages. Don't look upon Hebrew and Greek as burdensome courses you have to take, courses you'll be glad to forget a few years hence. If you want to lift your ministry above carbon-copy mediocrity, maintain a working knowledge of the original languages and keep using the tools.

That is not to say that Hebrew and Greek will solve all exegetical and theological problems, or that they alone will make you an effective preacher. Languages can create problems as well as solve them. But it is our feeling that some degree of competence in the originals gives enrichment and stability to a man's ministry. When he stands in the pulpit to deliver God's message, he at least knows that he has done his best with the text God gave him. Certainly he will use the best English translations, but he will also do word studies in the original and consult the scholarly texts for deeper truth. There are so many fine linguistic tools available these days that no minister ought to be satisfied with studying only the English text.

We have enjoyed comparing commentators, something you cannot do unless you maintain at least a working knowledge of the original languages. We will read Richard Lenski and get one meaning of the Greek, and then turn to William Hendriksen and find him, in a footnote, challenging Lenski's interpretation. Then we turn to the "old but good" commentators like Dean

Henry Alford and Joseph Lightfoot, only to discover additional data. Our own capabilities are slim, but we pity the minister who has no language training at all.

How do you hold on to language skills after you leave the classroom? Some professors will suggest that you read in the originals every day, if only a few verses. If you use the better commentaries, you will have to maintain a good working knowledge of Hebrew and Greek; but don't panic if you find yourself getting a bit rusty. Stay with it! You can always consult the grammars and other texts when you find you've forgotten some rule. The important thing is that you not waste what you have worked so hard to gain. Dr. George Morrison has a splendid sermon on Proverbs 12:27: "The slothful man roasteth not that which he took in hunting" (KJV). He entitled the sermon, "Wasted Gains." Imagine a hunter spending all day pursuing his game, catching it, and then not eating it! Well, imagine a student investing two or three years studying Hebrew and Greek, and then not using it!

Yes, there are effective preachers with big churches, who have never worried about Hebrew and Greek; so why should you? Each man has his own gift and his own ministry. But we still don't believe that ministerial success is a substitute for ministerial excellence. There are also men who *do* know their Hebrew and Greek, and they also have large ministries. The important thing is that a man give his best to his Lord and to his congregation. If the neglect of languages is an evidence of carelessness and laziness, then no amount of "success" will atone for it. The men who can do well on limited means ought to do even better with ample means.

If God has chosen to reveal Himself to us through the medium of languages, and if the knowledge of God is important at all, then it behooves us to get to know and use those languages with some degree of competence. The day will come when examinations in Greek and Hebrew will be past, and exegesis papers no longer required; *but then the real test will begin.* You will be sharing the inspired Word of God with needy people. Will you be able to do your best?

The Spirit of God rides most triumphantly in his own chariot.

Thomas Manton

As there is a foolish, so there is a wise ignorance; in not prying into God's ark, not inquiring into things not revealed. I would fain know all that I need, and all that I may: I leave God's secrets to Himself. It is happy for me that God makes me of His court though not of His council.

Joseph Hall

I am a Bible-bigot. I follow it in all things, both great and small.

John Wesley

Compare Scripture with Scripture. False doctrines, like false witnesses, agree not among themselves.

William Gurnall

I have sometimes seen more in a line of the Bible than I could well tell how to stand under, and yet another time the whole Bible hath been to me as dry as a stick.

John Bunyan

The Bible seems to have a line without a limit. In nature, we seem to be bounded by the horizon; yet who has measured its diameter, or laid his hand upon the sky line? We move towards it, yet we never get away from the center. It is the same with the Divine revelation. Its sky line recedes as we advance. The limit is visible yet unapproachable. We can get to the end of the chapters, yet we can never get to the end of the book.

Joseph Parker

But know this first of all, that no prophecy of Scripture is a matter of one's own interpretation, for no prophecy was ever made by an act of human will, but men moved by the Holy Spirit spoke from God.

2 Peter 1:20-21

11

"Herman Who?"

Hermeneutics—the science of literary interpretation, especially the interpretation of the Bible. The word comes from the Greek word that means "to interpret." You will find it in your Greek New Testament in John 1:38 and 42 and 9:7, as well as in Hebrews 7:2. Hermes was the messenger of the gods, the Greek equivalent of Mercury. He was the god of speech, writing, and traffic, which explains why busts of Mercury (or Hermes) stood at street corners to mark directions and boundaries. If you want to hear God speak from His Word with accuracy and power, you had better master the principles of biblical interpretation.

Most students, when surveyed a few years after graduation, state that their classes in Bible study proved to be among the most practical, if not *the* most useful, of all the courses they took in school. The reason is obvious: the minister must be a man of the Book, and anything that helps him better understand the Bible enables him to be a better minister both personally and in the pulpit. G. Campbell Morgan used to say that each church should be "The House of the Interpreter." (The allusion is to *Pilgrim's Progress,* a book worth reading.) People come to church to hear the Word explained and applied. That is what they need and that is what they have a right to receive.

As you progress through your ministerial studies, you will discover that your Bible contains truth on several levels. There is, of course, *historical truth,* because our faith is based on fact. Your courses in Bible history, archaeology, and language will give you the foundation needed in this area. It is an exciting thing to see how the historicity of the Bible is affirmed and reaffirmed by scholars.

There is also *doctrinal truth,* the truth we know about God and His great plan of salvation. Our aim in study is not to get acquainted with a dusty museum, but to become vitally related to the God who made us, saved us, and wants to enrich and use us.

Each doctrine you study is a key to open a new door of Christian experience. Phillips Brooks advised young pastors to "seize the human side of all divinity . . . and the divine side of all humanity." In other words, doctrinal truth must issue in *practical truth*. Behaving and believing must always go together. The Puritan preacher Thomas Adams quaintly said, "The Word of life may be so distorted from the life of the Word, till it becomes the food of death." That is a statement worth pondering.

But somewhere in here we have to make room for *devotional truth*. To quote another Puritan (and how the Puritans loved their Bibles!), "Read the Scripture, not only as a history, but as a love-letter sent to you from God." Thomas Watson said that, and saintly John Newton echoed it: "To read the Scripture, not as an attorney may read a will, merely to know the sense; but as the heir reads its, as a description and proof of his interest; to hear the Gospel as the voice of our Beloved." There is a time and place for exegesis, grammar, syntax, and all the valuable apparatus of linguistic scholarship; but there is also a time and place for opening the heart to God and receiving His Word as His voice to the inner man.

There are extremes that we must avoid, of course. In the hour of personal devotion, when hermeneutics and homiletics are chained outside the door, we must be careful not to become fanatics. God *does* speak to our hearts as we wait before Him. Some word given to Moses may come to our own souls with intense power. So be it. Personal experience and church history both bear witness that God impresses His will upon us through the Word. But we must guard against a mental dichotomy that subtly forces us to have two different Bibles, one for the head and one for the heart. The same Holy Spirit who teaches us the Word also wants to guide us into the perfect will of God.

In your classes on Bible study, you will use God's Word as a textbook; so be careful not to treat it like any other book. Granted, the Bible is a literary product—*the* greatest book in history—and therefore it can be subjected to the strictest literary analysis. But it is more than literature, and for that reason deserves reverence and respect beyond anything we would show to *The Iliad* or Shakespeare. First Thessalonians 2:13 is a good verse to memorize and heed whenever you approach your Bible merely as a textbook.

When a student begins to get involved in serious Bible study (as opposed to preparing a Sunday school lesson), he goes through several stages. First, he is excited by the new concepts and tools that are shared with him. But soon, that excitement is replaced by perplexity; for some of his cherished "interpretations" start to go right down the drain. He discovers that "study to shew thyself approved unto God" (2 Timothy 2:15, KJV) really has nothing to do with sitting in the library, and that the parables are much more than "earthly stories with heavenly meanings." Have his pastors and Sunday school teachers been wrong all these years? What *can* he believe about the Bible?

If you do reach that stage of perplexity, give yourself time and you will sooner or later come to a stage of maturity. Serious Bible study will no longer be a threat to your cherished opinions and traditions, nor will you be an iconoclast zealously attacking what you think is erroneous in other people's faith. The beautiful thing about the Bible is that it grows with us. "Nobody ever outgrows Scripture," said Charles Haddon Spurgeon; "the Book widens and deepens with our years." Of course, what you get out of *any* book, including the Bible, depends on what you bring to it; and that means not only a clear mind, but also a warm heart.

The principles of hermeneutics are not a threat to mature faith. They are a threat to a faith based on spiritualizing and allegorizing the sacred text, a faith built on types and symbols. But don't be afraid of taking down the scaffolding; it doesn't hold up the building anyway. Every ministerial student carries with him a certain amount of intellectual and religious rubbish that has to be discarded at one time or another if he is going to make progress. However, don't write home and tell your pastor he is a poor interpreter of the Word, or report to your parents that you have begun to question the notes in your study Bible. They will only react negatively and stop supporting the school, and your tuition will go up. Give yourself time to learn how to use these new tools with mature judgment, and things will go better for everybody.

One of the dangers of studying hermeneutics is the fear of misinterpreting the Word, a fear that could lead to paralysis. The Holy Spirit will never teach you from the Bible things that He did not put there. Again, time and maturity will help to solve the problem. Far better to approach the text with fear and trembling than to mangle it by assuming a know-it-all attitude.

Another danger is the smothering of imagination. Your analysis of Scripture can be so sterile that your sermons become dull lectures instead of satisfying spiritual meals. Since the Bible *is* literature—poetry, parable, metaphor, irony, satire, narrative are all there—we must make use of our sanctified imagination if we are to understand it and present its truths accurately. An outline is not a message any more than a recipe is a meal. Enter into the spirit of the text and prepare your message accordingly. The "courtroom" atmosphere of Romans is alien to the "holy of holies" atmosphere of Hebrews or the pastoral settings of many of the psalms. A wise use of the principles of hermeneutics will give you *information,* but you need to add *imagination* if your ministry is to be effective. It has well been said that the purpose of a sermon is not to discuss a subject, but to achieve an object; and that requires a certain amount of imagination.

This is a good place to discuss Bible translations. Some instructors prefer certain translations for class use, and you will have to conform. Many love the King James Version and would never say a disparaging word about it. But it is likely that you will select one of the modern translations for personal study and perhaps even for devotional reading. The important thing is that you ultimately select the translation that best fits you. No translation is without its faults (another reason for holding on to your Greek and Hebrew), and the best ones have varying merit. When you get into your own church, you will have to decide which version to use; and you will be careful not to upset the saints who think that the King James Version was brought down from heaven.

One of the great joys of ministry is the privilege of spending time digging into the treasures of the Word. The excited expositor can hardly wait to get into his study and open the Book and the books. The principles and tools of hermeneutics will be faithful servants if you will be faithful to them. You will be like that householder who knows just what to feed his family (Luke 12:42), or that steward who brought things new and old out of his vault (Matthew 13:52). Don't be tempted to look constantly for things new, because your people also need things old. The new comes out of the old and one strengthens the other.

When the Pilgrims left for America, their pastor, John Robinson, reminded them: "The Lord has more truth yet to break forth out of His holy Word."

"O send out Thy light and Thy truth, let them lead me" (Psalm 43:3).

Let us rejoice with one another that in a world where there are a great many good and happy things for men to do, God has given us the best and happiest, and made us preachers of His Truth.

Phillips Brooks

Oh, how I trembled when I was ascending the pulpit for the first time! I would feign have excused myself, but they made me preach.

Martin Luther

Do not regard preparations for the pulpit as a trifling thing; and do not rush upon your holy duties without devout preparation for the hallowed service. . . . Get your message fresh from God.

Charles Haddon Spurgeon

A preacher may not be a great man, but he must preach great matters. . . . To some men preaching is sailing on a puddle. . . . Daintiness would slur a sermon just as a pink ribbon would make a cannon appear ridiculous.

Bishop William Quayle

The supreme work of the Christian minister is the work of preaching. This is a day in which one of our greatest perils is that of doing a thousand little things to the neglect of the one thing, which is preaching.

G. Campbell Morgan

A work of compassion even of the most devoted and sacrificial kind tells nothing per se about the gospel of the kingdom of God. It only begins to speak of that when it is associated with, and interpreted by, the preaching of the gospel.

H. H. Farmer

I preached as never sure to preach again, and as a dying man to dying men.

Richard Baxter

The work of preaching is the highest and the greatest and the most glorious calling to which anyone can ever be called.

D. Martyn Lloyd-Jones

12

Preaching,
Pro and Con

"**P**reachers are born, not made," Dr. D. Martyn Lloyd-Jones affirms in his book *Preaching and Preachers*. "This is an absolute. You will never teach a man to be a preacher if he is not already one." But, since the good doctor made that statement first in a series of *seminary* lectures, we must believe that, somewhere in his heart, he found a place for ministerial education. We know of no contemporary preacher of stature who loved young ministers more, or who spent more time helping them, than Dr. Martyn Lloyd-Jones.

What he seems to be saying is, "You must have the gift from God if you are going to preach successfully. No amount of training or education can compensate for the lack of a spiritual gift. If you have the gift, others can help you develop it. If you don't have it, you are wasting your time."

Of course, the trembling seminary student stands there and wonders how he can discover this gift in time. Ideally, we ought to "find ourselves" as we serve in a local church; but some students who have a genuine "call" received that call while preparing for another career when still unconverted. Church history reminds us that some great preachers did not know their own gifts and had to be "thrown in the water" by others. John Knox and George W. Truett come to mind.

We think that it is indispensable for the preacher to have a divine call. It might not come in a dramatic way, but come it must. Knowing that God has called us to preach is a great encouragement to service and an equally great deterrant to carelessness and sin. If you are not excited about preaching God's Word, then it may be that preaching is not your calling and that He has some other kind of ministry for you.

We also think it is a good thing for a prospective preacher to

Take every opportunity you can for preaching experience.

get some experience in his own local church before he heads for the campus. Granted, that is not always possible; but it is desirable. In our own case, we each taught in Sunday school, tried to give "pep talks" in the youth group, helped in Vacation Bible School, and preached with fear and trembling at rescue missions before we ventured too far in ministerial training. It did us good.

Let's deal with some of the frustrations you might have in your classes on preaching.

First of all, you may have an instructor or two who really are not gifted preachers. Your immediate (and erroneous) response may be, "Well, what can *they* teach *me*?" The answer is: a great deal. There is both a *science* and an *art* to preaching, and you need to learn both. Many a homiletics professor knows his field exhaustively, but may not be able to preach like Spurgeon or one of your more modern homiletical heroes. He can still teach you the fundamentals of sermon preparation and take you a long way down the trail of developing your own gifts. The science of preaching is something you learn from a technician; the art of preaching is something you learn from a successful preacher, a role model. Don't confuse the two.

Your second frustration may well be with the homiletics course itself. "Why bother with all these principles and examples?" you argue. "The fire is burning in my soul and I don't feel any need to sit in class and study books and outlines." Well, it's a glorious thing to have the fire in your soul, if you keep a cool head. Even a fire needs to be controlled. The basics of sermon preparation are not unlike the scales that a musician must learn and practice before graduating to something higher. Once you learn the basics, you can improvise with greater success. Over the centuries, the masters of preaching have learned a few things; and you ought to be glad they are sharing them with you. After all, no surgeon would rush into the operating room without first having learned surgery; and all he can do is kill the body. *A man making a mess out of a sermon might destroy a soul for whom Christ died.* The work we are called to do is the highest and holiest possible, and we always want to do our best.

You may find yourself frustrated by having to preach in class. "Preaching to my peers is an artificial situation," you argue, "and having to watch myself on videotape makes it even worse." We sympathize with that attitude, but we don't totally agree with it. To begin with, you can always find some truth in the Bible that can be preached even to a class of seminarians. (How about, "Awake, thou that sleepest"?) Surely there is something in the Word that has helped you and is worth sharing with your fellow students. Furthermore, seeing yourself on an instant replay may be embarrassing, but it can be most helpful. Many of us have undetected mannerisms that ought to be eliminated as soon as possible. (When you get to be a great preacher someday, those mannerisms will be accepted as a part of your style, and younger students will imitate them. Meanwhile, try to get rid of them before you corrupt a whole new generation of preachers.)

Certainly it would be better if each student had a congregation to minister to week after week; but since not that many churches are available, we have to do the next best thing. However, that doesn't stop you from taking advantage of every preaching opportunity that comes your way, if it doesn't seriously interfere with your classwork. The art of preaching is learned by preaching and by listening to other men preach, so get all the experience you can.

One of the major frustrations of homiletics students is the feeling that the instructor is trying to put each of them into the same mold. Each instructor has his own style and approach, and perhaps his own role models that have meant a great deal to him. Your style may be different, and you may have questions about his approach. Don't get upset. Like the piano teacher, your instructor has to start you off on the basics *as he knows them*; but the wise teacher will quickly recognize true ability when he sees it reflected in creative work. The senior member of this team has taught homiletics and knows how difficult it is to evaluate sermon outlines. Give your instructor the benefit of the doubt, but don't hesitate to chat with him privately if you think you have a grievance.

It may take you a few years in your own church before you will really discover and discipline your own special gifts. Be patient. God wants you to preach *your way,* not somebody else's way; but be sure that "your way" is really your best. There is a great gulf fixed between "novelty" and "creativity," and blessed is the preacher who knows which side he is on. Once you have mastered the traditional, you will be at liberty to experiment as the Lord gives you direction.

You will probably be asked to read a lot of sermons. Be sure you read them *as a Christian needing nourishment,* and not as a critic. After you have digested the food, then you can debate with the cook. Most of the sermons you read may not be "your kind of preaching," but don't reject them for that reason. The printed sermons that have stood the test of time have something to teach you, so take them seriously. Adopt the same attitude toward chapel speakers and other preachers you may hear from time to time. The sermons of master preachers, some deceased, are available on tape and are probably in your school library. Learn to be a good listener. The main thing is not to say, "I wouldn't do it that way!" but to ask, "Now, why did he do it *that* way?" Learn to separate the essentials from the accidentals. Master preachers occasionally break the rules, but they *know* they are breaking the rules and *why* they are doing it.

Be sure that you participate in every seminary class *as a preacher of the Word.* Start now to develop a homiletical viewpoint in your studies. You are not just a theology student; you are *a preacher* studing theology. You are not a history student; you are *a preacher* studying church history. This is not to say that you spend all your time looking for sermon ideas or illustrations; but it does mean that you approach your studies with the view of making them *practical.* "Where does this truth (or fact) touch life?" is a good question to keep before you in every class. Your instructor may not have had pastoral or preaching experience, but that need not hinder you from seeing the course from a practical viewpoint.

You may want to start a sermon notebook, in which you jot down ideas that come to you at unexpected times. If a certain text hits you with unusual power, write it down and meditate on it. Mark in your textbooks or notes those items that have particular application to preaching and pastoral work. One of the exciting trends in practical theology today is the emphasis on biblical theology, basing the ministry on what God has revealed in His Word. The best writers in this field are not just compiling notes on "how to do it in the church." Rather, they are first explaining *why* we do it that way. The "theology of ministry" that is developing today is but another proof that all truth is interrelated.

We hope that at least one of your instructors will discuss the sermon as an act of worship. It is too bad that some textbooks divorce preaching from the total life of the church and the total context of the worship service. Any instructor who tells you that whatever goes on before the sermon is but preliminaries had better take a course in the meaning of worship. Certainly, preaching is central; churches don't grow and Christians don't get strengthened by short devotional talks tacked at the end of a concert. But the fact that the sermon is central need not mean that everything else is peripheral. Singing, praying, reading the Scriptures, giving, and even waiting in silence, can all be a part of fellowship with God and witness to a lost world. We wish that each ministerial student would be required to take at least one course in worship, taught by an instructor who knows the total context of the local church. It might make a difference in the way we prepare our services *and* our sermons.

Don't be discouraged if your progress in preaching seems to be slow. Just make sure you are going in the right direction—discovering your own gifts and learning how best to use them. After he had been preaching in London for many years, Spurgeon confessed that he was still learning how to preach. We feel sorry for the congregation whose pastor is sure he has arrived. There is always something new to learn in the vast field of communicating the Word to modern man.

In one sense, preaching is not *taught*—it is *caught*. Happy is that student who somewhere meets a teacher or preacher who lights a fire in his soul. Unless you are motivated by "Woe is me if I do not preach the gospel" (1 Corinthians 9:16), you will not last very long. The church is waiting for preachers and desperately needs preachers more than she realizes. On those gloomy days when you feel like giving up, ponder these words of a master preacher, A. J. Gossip, in his book *In Christ's Stead:*

> But always it has been through preaching that revivals have come: always by preaching that the Spirit has made the tired Church young again. No bustle of energy can do it, no whirring of machinery, sending a gale into our tired faces, no endless and elaborate organization, no, and no glory of art.

Preaching is a manly calling. It will demand the best you have. "It takes more courage to be a preacher," wrote Bishop William Quayle, "than to be a gladiator, or a stormer of fortresses, because the preacher's battle is ever on, never ceases, and lacks the tonic of visible conquest." Give it your best now, and you will do your best when God gives you opportunities to preach His Word.

All effective preaching is to the individual.

I live for souls and for eternity, I want to win some soul to Christ. If you want this and work for it, eternity alone can tell the result.

Dwight L. Moody

A man, who had his eyes up to heaven, the best of books was in his hand, the law of truth was written upon his lips, and he stood as if he pleaded with men.

John Bunyan

Ignorance is not a qualification for evangelism. My dear young brother, are you looking forward to an evangelistic ministry? Then I plead with you, gird up the loins of your mind, and obtain all the knowledge possible. No single branch of knowledge is out of place to the man who is going to do the work of an evangelist.

G. Campbell Morgan

It must be heart-work with you, brethren, far more than head-work, if you are to win many souls. Amidst all your studies, mind you that you never let your spiritual life get dry. . . . Do not be satisfied with merely polishing up your grates, but stir the fire in your heart, and get your own soul all aflame with love to Christ, or else you will not be likely to be greatly used in the winning of the souls of others.

Charles Haddon Spurgeon

Pay close attention to yourself and to your teaching; persevere in these things; for as you do this you will insure salvation both for yourself and for those who hear you.

1 Timothy 4:16

To evangelize is so to present Christ Jesus in the power of the Holy Spirit that men shall come to put their trust in God through Him, to accept Him as their Saviour, and serve Him as their King in the fellowship of His Church.

Toward the Conversion of England
The Archbishop's Commission on
Evangelism

13

Evangelism and Missions

When the Great Exhibition of the Works of Industry of All Nations was opened in 1851 by Queen Victoria, people flocked to Hyde Park to behold the marvels of the modern age. Steam was the magic word—steam plows, steam locomotives, steam looms, steam organs, even a steam cannon. And there were prizes for great achievements, like the sportsman's knife with eighty blades, and (our favorite) a gadget that did absolutely nothing, but it had seven thousand parts. It actually won a prize!

On that basis, many churches today could win prizes: they have thousands of moving parts, but nothing is being accomplished. The machinery moves smoothly and the operators and investors are pleased, but no products are being displayed.

Perhaps you heard about the little lady from Iowa who was part of a group touring Westminster Abbey. When the tour was over, as is the custom, the guide asked, "Are there any questions?" The lady from Iowa spoke up, "Has anybody been saved here lately?"

The church exists, not for itself, but for ministry to a lost world. One of the most difficult battles you may fight during your school career (depending, perhaps, on the school you attend) is the maintaining of a burden for the lost. Some schools major on evangelism (or "soul winning") and keep the fire burning. Other campuses raise their students to be somewhat skeptical of aggressive evangelism. It is unfortunate when a style of evangelism, or a methodology, becomes a test of fellowship and spirituality. But it is also unfortunate when an overreaction to the wrong kind of evangelism helps to put the fire out. Jesus wept over lost people, and you dare not ignore them.

The other extreme, of course, is to go on a guilt trip and make a nuisance of yourself. We doubt that a feeling of guilt is the best motive for witnessing and seeking to lead others to the Savior. Paul hit the highest motive for evangelism when he wrote, "For the love of Christ controls us" (2 Corinthians 5:14). There is a difference between witnessing for Christ as Christian ambassadors and practicing "Christian salesmanship" in order to win converts.

You also want to avoid the snare of statistics. Only God knows how many of our "converts" are truly His children. That is no excuse for doing nothing, of course; but it is a warning against undue boasting. "I am not among those who decry statistics," Spurgeon told his students, "not do I consider that they are productive of all manner of evil; for they do much good if they are accurate, and if men use them lawfully." Often, those who criticize statistics have none to report.

It is unfortunate that some schools have dropped their required courses in evangelism. If you can fit a course in as an elective, do so. Even if you do, you may also want to attend a good seminar on evangelism. Many of the principles that have been effective in parachurch ministries will work successfully in the local church. As a shepherd, you need to learn how to increase your flock through spiritual births.

In the long run, evangelism that is related to the local church is the most economical and the most effective. To quote Spurgeon again: "Christian labors, disconnected from the church, are like sowing and reaping without having any barn in which to stow the fruits of the harvest; they are useful, but incomplete." The church that grows only by transferring members from other churches is not really fulfilling its mission on earth. That kind of "growth" has been compared to borrowing bricks from another building, or dipping fish out of another aquarium.

Cultivate a concern for the lost, and use the opportunities God gives you to share Christ with others. Even though you may live in a "Christian community" on campus, you will still have opportunities to witness to the lost; so stay alert. Don't advertise your burden, and don't boast about your "converts." Just do the job. God may bring to your side some students of like concern, and the result might well be revival on campus. Graduation and ordination will not make you a soul-winner. Only God can make you effective in the harvest, and He wants to start now.

In some schools, you do not get courses in missions unless you are majoring in that field. Try to take some courses as electives. We feel that a basic introduction to missions is important for pastoral ministry. If you minister in the city, you may find yourself on a mission field with a cross-cultural situation not unlike what your missionaries face overseas!

A knowledge of the history of missions and the principles of missionary ministry are important to the pastor who wants to lead his church in obeying Christ's commission. Missions and evangelism are not topics that we preach about; they are the circulatory system of every message, the heartbeat of every business meeting. Being "evangelical" should also mean being "evangelistic." If we really believe the gospel, and our own lives have been changed by Christ, then we must have an inner compulsion to share the message with others. No matter what doctrine you are preaching, you must always preach Christ; and to preach Christ means to tell the good news and encourage God's people to share that good news.

Some young ministers feel threatened by the media ministry. There is no need to fear; no media ministry will ever take the place of a local church. We thank God for all who sincerely preach the gospel and who seek to exalt Christ. We are not competing with each other, even though we may not always agree with everything we see and hear in media witness. Surveys indicate that the unsaved and unchurched, for the most part, are not being reached by the TV evangelists; so there are still plenty of fish to catch. The ministry of the local church is still God's number-one way to witness to the lost world; but let's be thankful for those who help us to witness, even if we may not totally agree with them.

While you are in school, get to know the veteran missionaries who may visit the campus or possibly serve on the faculty. It is helpful to see the missionary enterprise from the missionary's point of view. It would be helpful if each ministerial student could, during his years of training, actually visit a mission field and serve for a few months. If such an opportunity comes along, take advantage of it! It will enrich your life and ministry. That is not to suggest that a summer in Zaire will make you an expert, but it will open your eyes and touch your heart in ways that no amount of lecturing could do.

Dr. Oswald J. Smith has said, "The light that shines the farthest will shine the brightest at home." The church that has a concern for a lost world certainly ought to have a concern for its own neighbors. (The reverse is not always true. We know some large evangelistic churches that have a minimal missionary budget. But we also know some "missionary-minded churches" that have very little in the way of local evangelism. Blessed are the balanced.)

So many new and creative things are being done these days both in evangelism and missions that you must do your best to stay abreast of the action. Like some of us, you may say, "But I don't have a gift of evangelism." That may be so, but each minister is still commanded to "do the work of an evangelist" (2 Timothy 4:5). You may not be called to a mission field, but you must still focus the attention of your church on a world that needs Christ.

The church whose heart beats with a passion for souls will experience the working of the Spirit in wonderful ways. Pray for the lost; cultivate a burden for the lost; witness to the lost; preach to the lost. Encourage your people to witness. Don't be afraid of criticism. People who are busy serving Christ don't have time to criticize. "Therefore knowing the fear of the Lord, we persuade men" (2 Corinthians 5:11).

We suggest that you read *The Soul Winner,* by Charles Haddon Spurgeon (Grand Rapids: Eerdmans, 1963), one of the best books on evangelism from a pastor's point of view. *I Believe in Evangelism,* by David Watson (Grand Rapids: Eerdmans, 1976) is an excellent survey, and so also is *I Believe in the Great Commission,* by Max Warren (Grand Rapids: Eerdmans, 1976). There are scores of books available on various methods and techniques of evangelism and church missionary programs, but these books will give you the theology behind the methodology. That is important.

All men who are eminently useful, are made to feel their weakness in a supreme degree.

Charles Haddon Spurgeon

Thou hast commanded that an ill-regulated mind should be its own punishment.

St. Augustine

It is in that stubborn staying power most preachers fail. Gradually, imperceptibly, they lose heart and expectancy, come at last to put things through with the feeling it had better be done, but nothing much will come of it.

A. J. Gossip

It is not the number of books you read, nor the variety of sermons you hear, nor the amount of religious conversation in which you mix, but it is the frequency and earnestness with which you meditate on these things till the truth in them becomes your own and part of your being, that ensures your growth.

F. W. Robertson

The object of education is to prepare the young to educate themselves throughout their lives.

Robert Maynard Hutchins

From the cowardice that shrinks from new truth,
From the laziness that is content with half-truths,
From the arrogance that thinks it knows all truth,
    O God of truth, deliver us.

Ancient prayer

Every one should keep a mental waste-paper basket and the older he grows the more things he will consign to it—torn up to irrecoverable tatters.

Samuel Butler

Whatever is formed for long duration arrives slowly to its maturity.

Samuel Johnson

14

Measuring Yourself and Your Ministry

Perhaps you read about the man who purchased an economy car and boasted that he would get the best mileage of anybody in the office. And he did—for two months—because some of the men were secretly adding fuel to his gas tank. His mileage record was worthy of sending to the *Guiness Book of Records*. But then the rascals started to *siphon out* the gas, and that was the end of the great mileage record.

Even apart from the pranks that people can play on us, it is a difficult thing to measure performance, especially our own. Spurgeon used to go home and weep over what he felt were poor sermons, poorly delivered, only to learn later that God had used them to save sinners. More than one pastor has offered to resign, only to be told by his people that they felt his ministry was being blessed of God and that he ought to stay.

One of the greatest helps to an effective ministry (and a longer pastorate) is the ability to measure ourselves and our ministry. When the pastor and the church have different standards of measurement, you can expect conflict; and, when the pastor uses standards different from those that God uses, you can expect discouragement or a false confidence that leads to defeat.

We have suggested several times in this book that we must not measure the ministry by the same standards used in the business or professional world. (That does not mean we must not be businesslike in our work or unprofessional in our operation.) Stores can count customers and profits from sales; factories can count orders and shipments sent out; farmers can measure their crops and add up their profits or losses; but ministers and churches can't always measure progress or decline with such mathematical precision. Whether we like it or not, there are times when a *loss* of members is a better sign of progress than an addition of members!

The minister can tell he is growing when his mind and heart are open to truth and he is excited about discovering God's message in God's Word. He is willing to face problems honestly and seek God's will in solving them. He is relating creatively to his people so that they are not a threat to him but, instead, a challenge for him to do his best. That doesn't mean that he never has hours or days of discouragement. Even our Lord said to His disciples, "How long shall I be with you, and put up with you?" (Luke 9:41). But it does mean that he sees opportunities more than obstacles, and that he has the faith to believe that God is leading and will give the church victory.

The man or woman who says, "I have my education, so I am all set for life!" is destined for defeat. No matter how much education and training you have been privileged to receive, all of it is only a foundation for further growth and experience. As we have stated in a previous chapter, the day will come when you will lovingly toss some of your class notes into the wastebasket simply because you have grown out of them and have grown into something better. The fact that you are willing to learn something new and unlearn something old is proof that you are growing.

The growing minister comes to understand himself and his work better. He is not threatened by things he can't do or ministries that others can do better. He knows himself, and he is willing to be himself. Over the years, he sheds certain activities that don't belong to his life and ministry. Many of us were "all things to all men" as we got started in the Lord's work—we did youth work, spoke at camps, addressed sleepy people at banquets, preached evangelistic crusades, served on denominational and civic committees, and used every word in our vocabulary except "No!" Then we realized that God had certain tasks for *us* to perform, and that our eagerness to do everything for everybody only robbed others of the work God had for them to do. The maturing minister knows himself and gives his best self *to his best work*.

Nobody matures *alone* when it comes to the work of God. You need your church and the fellowship of other servants of God. We pity the pastor who knows so much that he can't learn anything from his own people. The familiar confession of Mark Twain comes to mind: "When I was a boy of fourteen, my father was so ignorant I could hardly stand to have the old man around. But when I got to be twenty-one, I was astonished at how much the old man had learned in seven years."

Become a part of some kind of ministerial fellowship that does more than hold business meetings and drink coffee. Get involved in the kind of discussions that will stretch your mind, even if you have to organize it yourself. If necessary, find a like-minded pastor and suggest that you read the same books and discuss them once a month, and then pray together. It is unfortunate that even denominational ministeriums often degenerate into promotional meetings when they ought to be arenas for intellectual and spiritual exercise.

We have already suggested that you should keep up with your Hebrew and Greek (and any other languages you have studied), so there is no need to go into that again. Watch the advertising in the best religious periodicals so you can keep abreast of the books being published in this area of study. The average Christian bookstore caters to the popular reader in the general public, so you may not find your scholarly tools there, although the manager would be more than happy to order books for you. If you are near a good theological library, visit it occasionally just to see what is being published, or what past publications you may have missed. While you are at it, don't bypass the local public library. A few hours a week browsing among the magazines and the new releases may be more enlightening than attending a theological lecture.

Set up a reading program for yourself and don't be detoured from it by every "best seller" that you see advertised. If you need help in the area of liberal arts, secure a copy of *The Lifetime Reading Plan,* by Clifton Fadiman (New York: Crowell, rev. ed., 1978). The classics that the author recommends will enrich your thinking and your preaching. We have appended a list of books that might be helpful to you, but these titles must not be construed as "the best" in any sense of the word. They are books that relate to ministry that have been helpful to us at one time or another. Books are something like garments; at one stage in life, you may be too small for them, and at another stage, too large. Each minister will have his own list of favorites, so please don't criticize our choices if they disagree with yours.

It may seem strange, but one evidence of growth in the ministry is an emerging awareness of your own insufficiency. Recently an assistant pastor said, "I had no idea that so much was involved in the ministry! At one time, I thought I was up to it; but now I'm not so sure!" Welcome to the club! "And who is adequate for these things?" asked Paul; and then he gave the answer: "Not that we are adequate in ourselves to consider anything as coming from ourselves, but our adequacy is from God, who also made us adequate as servants of a new covenant" (2 Corinthians 2:16 and 3:5-6). Perhaps our posture ought to be that of Jeremiah: bold before men, but broken before God.

If Romans 8:28 means anything at all, it means that we need not fall apart at the crises we face in our own lives and in the church. It is certainly a mark of maturity that the minister constantly faces new and more complex problems and does not look for either easy solutions (that only create more problems) or handy escape hatches. It has often been said that a crisis does not make a man; it shows what a man is made of. No minister enjoys parish problems or personal problems, but neither does he complain about them or try to run away to a better church. There are problems in *every* church, because churches are made up of people; and the pastor who flees to what he thinks is a safer place only discovers that he has brought the most dangerous thing with him—the fear and unbelief in his own heart.

Often a maturing ministry of the Word in a local church only reveals new problems, and that in itself is an encouragement. During our early years of ministry in a church, we discover the surface problems, the situations that are only symptoms of much deeper needs. The longer we stay, the deeper the Word probes, and the more the enemy fights us. People who have been officers perhaps for years suddenly decide to resign, or perhaps they even leave the church. Is this a sign of failure on the part of the minister? Not necessarily. However, he should deal with each situation personally, in depth, and try to help the person discover what the real problem is.

Where there is life, there has to be growth. No minister is satisfied with a family that doesn't reproduce. Sometimes it takes a few years to clean away the debris and prepare the way, but ultimately there has to be increase: "fruit . . . more fruit . . . much fruit" (John 15:2, 5). One pastor faithfully ministered for five years and there seemed to be very little fruit for his labor, but then the harvest came; and now he is working overtime to conserve the results. Not every church will be huge, because not every pastor is equipped to serve a huge church; but

"We interrupt this wedding to find out what we are supposed to be doing."

every church should grow and seek to reach its potential to the glory of God.

As you try honestly to measure your ministry, ask yourself:

1. Are the people in my church discovering and developing their spiritual gifts?

2. Is there a place for everybody? Are more people getting involved in the ministry?

3. Am I working myself out of jobs or taking on more jobs?

4. Are all of us becoming more like Jesus Christ?

5. Is the Bible, or the church constitution, governing the life of the church? Are we depending on rules and regulations or on the life of the Spirit as He teaches us from the Word?

6. Is God meeting our needs in answer to prayer?

7. Am I ministering by faith, or do I "scheme" to get things accomplished?

8. Are more people ministering effectively to each other? Is there a growing sense of unity in the fellowship?

9. Have we dared to scrap some dead ministries and start some new ones, or are we monitoring conformity?

10. Does our church have its own distinctive ministry, or are we slavishly imitating some other church?

11. Are people amazed at what is happening? Do they give God the glory? "If you can explain what's happening, God probably didn't do it."

12. Is our church a witnessing community outside the walls of the building? Does the unsaved crowd think we are drunk—or dead?

13. Are we moving into exciting "pioneer territory," or are we fishing in the same puddles with the same bait?

14. Do the people have a healthy appetite for the Word? Are they willing to move into different "pastures" as I lead them in the study of Scripture?

15. Are there more opportunities than workers?

16. Is the Spirit calling out workers from our fellowship to serve Him elsewhere, *perhaps even in other churches in the area?*

17. Am I comfortable in my work and able to handle it with ease, or am I having to confess my need for more of God's help? Is the challenge gone?

18. Is the Lord giving us new ideas? Are we afraid to change?

As you take inventory of your personal life, you might ask:

1. Is my personal devotional life really satisfying, or just

routine? Is God answering *specific* prayers?

2. Do my wife and I agree on ministry, or are there tensions?

3. Are there any growing problems with the children that are directly related to ministry?

4. Am I giving my family a negative view of the church and the ministry? Do they see me *enjoying* or *enduring* the ministry?

5. Am I still willing to make sacrifices for the work, or am I handing in petty expense accounts?

6. Am I watching the clock and the calendar, just living for the end of the workday and the weekly day off? Am I "instant in season, out of season," or putting in an eight-hour day?

7. Am I bothered when people make demands on me, when I am interrupted? Are the same people getting on my nerves?

8. Am I prone to put people off or give them "stock answers" to their problems?

9. Am I willing to stay here and serve faithfully until God moves me elsewhere, or am I looking at "greener pastures" somewhere else?

10. Is there authority in my preaching because I really seek to teach the Word and practice it myself?

We could add more questions, but we're sure you get the idea. Socrates said that the unexamined life was not worth living, and we say that the unexamined ministry is not worth maintaining. A growing knowledge of yourself and your work is essential to an effective ministry to the glory of God. However, keep in mind that your own self-examination could occasionally be wrong! If you find yourself discouraged because of some weakness or failure, before you consider resigning, talk it over with your wife, a fellow pastor, or a trusted confidant in the church. Take a day off, get some extra sleep, get away from the battlefield, spend extra time in the Word and prayer, and give God an added opportunity to talk to you.

Finally, keep in mind that only God knows the human heart, and that the final evaluation rests with Him. John the Baptist, languishing in prison, was sure he was a failure; but Jesus called him the greatest of the prophets! Take heart!

The certainties of one age are the problems of the next.
Richard H. Tawney

All that is human must retrograde if it does not advance.
Edward Gibbon

So, there is nothing new under the sun.
Ecclesiastes 1:9

> Change and decay in all around I see;
> O Thou, who changest not, abide with me!
> *H. F. Lyte*

The art of progress is to preserve order amid change and to preserve change amid order.
Alfred North Whitehead

Nothing is permanent but change.
Heraclitus

Somehow the top of our existence seems to be severed from its roots in a deeper level of reality, so that it lacks a consistent substructure to hold it together, with the result that so often today the creative forces in human life seem to be fighting a losing battle against the forces of fragmentation and disintegration.
Thomas F. Torrance

15

Thinking About Today

Today's young pastor confronts a different world from that which his father confronted a generation ago. To be sure, sin is still the same, and the grace of God has not changed; but there is a different atmosphere and attitude abroad.

For one thing, people are openly discussing subjects that, a generation ago, were kept under wraps. Sad to say, open discussion sometimes means open practice. Perhaps the news coverage is just better today, but it sees like more people are getting involved in more wrong things than ever before. People seem more materialistic. "Practical atheism" is the phrase that would best describe most of our neighbors, including many professed Christians. They say they believe in God, but their real "god" is the car in the garage (now costing more than ever to run), the TV set, the boat, the snowmobile, and the fringe benefits. If a child doesn't have an electronic arcade in his bedroom, he thinks he's been deprived.

At the same time, we have an economic crunch, a lot of people hungry and unemployed, and the "American Way of Life" being challenged by erosion inside the country and enemies outside the country. Daily survival is more important to most people than peace in the Mideast or *détente* with Russia. Today's pastor must minister to people whose minds are divided. On the one hand, Christians want to be spiritual and serve God; but on the other hand, they are pressured to conform and to take care of "number one."

Suspicion is the dark cloud that overshadows much of life. People don't have confidence in any kind of authority. This is a backlash from Vietnam, Watergate, Abscam, and a host of lesser incidents that make *integrity* an outdated word. Add to that the propaganda that comes from some media ministry, and it isn't difficult to understand why people don't want to trust authority.

The so-called old-fashioned values are rapidly deteriorating. Marriage is no longer a lifetime commitment to God and to your mate. People want a "trial marriage" before they take the plunge; and, if it doesn't work out even then, they get a divorce and start over with a new partner. It's for better or for worse, but not for long. One pastor reported that three of his last four weddings involved partners already living together.

Children grow up in homes where there is little discipline. Parents who can't control themselves have a hard time controlling their offspring. Society emphasizes enjoyment, not enrichment. "Have fun now—pay later!" The young pastor tries to share eternal values with people whose greatest concern is immediate prices. We don't find many people like Abraham and Moses who turn their backs on immediate achievement in order to trust God and please Him.

We have all accepted the fact that we live in a pluralistic society, with all of the strengths and weaknesses that involves. We have learned to accept (or at least tolerate) other ethnic and religious groups; but the trouble is, people now have the idea that *all* religions are equal, so there is no need to preach the gospel. Your neighbor's faith is just as good as yours, even though your neighbor may be building his faith on ignorant superstition. It has become unpatriotic to share your faith.

Our cities are in trouble, and churches are fleeing the cities to find refuge in the suburbs. But our suburbs are also in trouble. The city church that doesn't learn to get along with its neighbors is doomed, and the suburban church that ignores the needs of the city is blind and missing a great opportunity.

As never before, the pastor must keep up with things. Congress now debates matters that impinge upon ethics: abortion, euthanasia, test-tube babies, genetic engineering, and other issues. Who determines what is right and what is wrong? Are some actions legal but not scriptural? Are some actions illegal and scriptural? The church has moved into the political arena with mixed results. We may have won some elections and lost some spiritual power.

We are bombarded daily with media messages of one kind or another, and most people don't realize how all of this affects their thinking. There have been personal and cultural pressures ever since Adam and Eve left the Garden; but today, we share the problems of a whole world *right in our own living room*. The consequences of "future shock" may already be upon us—heart attacks, high blood pressure, ulcers, nervous indecision, and the frightening feeling that you really have no control over your own life. Today's pastor must minister in an anxious world to people who desperately need help, more than they realize themselves.

But there are some good signs!

One of them is the growing involvement of the laity in the ministry. (We don't like that word *laity*, but it's the best word available at present.) It is encouraging to see programs for the training of church members—teaching, soul-winning, discipleship, stewardship, administration, family leadership, and so on. The old attitude, "We have a pastor and pay him—let *him* do the work!" has been replaced with a new attitude of pastor and people working together. The pastor is a "playing coach" on the team, and he can learn from others as well as teach others.

Of course, there is a danger here, especially where you have some gifted laymen who are not called to full-time ministry. They might get the idea that the pastor is a fifth wheel and not really needed. But the risk is worth taking; the trained church member is a mighty weapon in the hands of God. Pastors come and go, but the dedicated officer stays to keep the church moving in the right direction.

There seems to be more interest in the Bible these days, even in churches that once officially resisted Bible study. The home Bible study groups have led many to Christ and helped many believers face and solve problems on the basis of Bible truth. The emphasis on expository preaching is an encouragement to any pastor who loves the Word and enjoys expounding it. A wealth of helpful literature is available for the advanced layman who wants to have a working knowledge of the Bible. The popularity of certain media preachers, and the availability of cassettes, is both a help and a problem to the pastor: a help, in that these ministries give the believer more of the Word; a problem, in that the believers may depend more on a distant media preacher than on their own pastor. In the end, it probably balances out.

Churches are learning to diversify. They have discovered that the Body must be flexible. Along with the traditional ministries, churches are daring to do some new things in both evangelism and Christian education. Of course, we have had our share of transient novelties; but that should not stifle our creativity. The

Holy Spirit of God is infinitely original!

Thanks to good books and magazines, the average church member can find out what Christian leaders are thinking and saying, what the problems are, and what each Christian can do about them. In fact, in some churches, some of the members are better prepared to discuss these issues than their pastor is! But it is a good thing that the church is openly discussing things like inerrancy, social justice, pacifism, the Christian and culture, ecumenism, and so on. We may never reach final agreement on any of these issues. But it does us good to discuss them and be informed. The abused word *dialogue* sometimes means "compromise," but it can also mean a kind of creative confrontation that does everybody good (except the man with a closed mind).

It is encouraging to see that "small" is beautiful again— small cars, small houses and apartments, small stores, and small churches. We get the impression that thinking Christians are wanting to identify with caring fellowships and not just big crowds. We thank God for every church, large or small, that preaches the Word; but we wonder if people who are lonely and needy aren't seeking a closer fellowship with other believers. It is also encouraging to see that the larger churches are organizing "circles of concern," care groups that can meet the needs of people individually. We feel there is a real future for the smaller neighborhood church and that those churches will meet needs that perhaps the larger ministries might not meet.

Another encouragement is the emphasis on visitation, ministering in the home, not just to witness to the lost or reclaim the wandering, but also to encourage the faithful and share the burdens with the whole family. We wonder how the pastor who never visits or counsels is able to prepare messages that really meet the needs of his people. How difficult it would be to preach to *strangers* week after week! We need pastoral specialists, but we also need the "general practitioner" who can apply the Word in many areas of life. We think the time is coming when "expert exposition" in the pulpit will not be enough to meet all the problems people face. They will need the personal care of the shepherd as well.

The younger pastor and his wife can be thankful that the pastoral "fishbowl" has been broken, and they and their children can live normal lives. It used to be common for a local church (or board) to "own" the pastor's family as well as the residence, but things are different now. Without minimizing the importance of being good examples to the flock, the shepherd and shepherdess today are more free to have a life-style that is not of the traditional "fishbowl" variety. The pastor's wife can even be gainfully employed! A generation ago, this would have been cited as evidence that she had no faith in God or love for the church. Today, the working women in the church welcome her into the club and praise her. It is not unusual for churches to permit the pastor to own his own home, a practice that we feel is a good one.

However, the demands of ministry today are such that the young pastor, in his quest for success in church, had better beware lest he fail at home. The increase in the clergy divorce rate is alarming. The minister who cares for his family is at the same time caring for the church, because his family is a part of the church.

Is there a temptation today to minimize the pulpit? We think so. Our people hear so much "talk" in the course of a day, much of it propaganda, that they really don't know how to listen to a sermon. Somebody runs off to a conference or seminar and comes back with a new scheme to convert the neighborhood through films, music, cassettes, or religious drama, and the preacher again feels threatened. There is no substitute for preaching. Put your best work into the pulpit ministry, and those auxiliary ministries will take care of themselves. One pastor we know asked his people to listen to his messages for six months before coming to him for counseling, and many of the people discovered God had met their needs. A famous pastor said that the test of a good sermon was the number of people who wanted to see him during the week. We wonder if the test of a good sermon might not be the number who decide they *don't* have to see the pastor!

One serious problem these days is the brevity of the average pastorate. Men are not "staying by the stuff" and seeing a local church through to new growth and strength. Worse yet, too many men are leaving the ministry when the going gets tough. Perhaps some of them should never have entered the ministry to begin with, but that doesn't lessen the seriousness of the problem. The pressures in the ministry today are tremendous, and only the grace of God and the prayers and love of God's people can see a man through. Fortunately, times have changed, and the pastor no longer has to stand piously on a pedestal. He can honestly share his burdens and frustrations with his people and they will love him for it. Some men are too proud to be vulnerable, and they are usually the ones who crack.

When you get right down to it, times have always been tough. You can quote Charles Dickens and apply it to almost any period in history: "It was the best of times, it was the worse of times, it was the age of wisdom, it was the age of foolishness, it was the epoch of belief, it was the epoch of incredulity." The minister who complains about the times is often only looking for an excuse for his own failure. Paul had the right approach: "But I shall remain in Ephesus until Pentecost; for a wide door for effective service has opened to me, and there are many adversaries" (1 Corinthians 16:8-9). Unbelief sees the obstacles, but faith sees the opportunities along with the obstacles.

This much is sure: the world today needs pastoral ministry. Only God, working through His church, can solve the problems that people face today. It's a privilege to be in His service and to be a part of the answer, not a part of the problem.

We pray God's richest blessing on you and your ministry!

16

Some Modest Suggestions to Those in Charge of Ministerial Training

To begin with, we want to assure you that we are not among the number who take great delight in criticizing schools, particularly seminaries. That seems to be a popular activity these days, but we are not trying to encourage it.

However, we do feel that anything that man does is always capable of improvement, and that includes ministerial education. It is in the spirit of Ephesians 4:15, "speaking the truth in love," that we make these modest suggestions.

1. *Encourage the integrating of the various disciplines so that the student can more easily see the total picture of ministry to the church.*

One of the easiest ways to do this is to have some team-teaching in different classes, bringing the practical theology department and the other departments together. Let the preacher and the professor together teach both exegesis and exposition.

If the dean cannot schedule team-teaching, then let the instructors visit each other's classes from time to time and make their contribution. Just as soon as a student learns what true exegesis is, he ought to be shown how it can be turned into nourishing messages for the church family. The young theologian, having studied the doctrine of the church, ought to be shown what this doctrine means in practical application.

Some instructors have had considerable pastoral experience and can do both jobs (the theoretical and the practical) themselves; but this kind is scarce. There ought to be enough honesty and humility in the hearts of faculty members that they would eagerly share what they know with each other and with the students. Occasional faculty forums on pertinent topics might encourage that kind of interdisciplinary cooperation.

It wouldn't hurt to have an orientation course early in the curriculum to explain to the new student some of the things we have shared in this book. Ideally, the course would involve a working pastor as well as instructors from both the practical and the academic sides of the fence. Give the new students some insight into what theological education and ministerial training are all about. Ask the Christian education department to develop some audiovisual tools so that the material can be dramatized. You might even bring in a young pastor, fresh on the field, who can give the latest battle statistics.

That is probably asking too much, but would it be possible also to have a similar short-term seminar at the close of their academic career? They had better know how to put things together before they graduate! If your school has a chaplain with pastoral experience, he might even counsel with each graduate personally.

We suggest that the dean of education survey the graduates one year after graduation, and ask them for their suggestions. The survey ought to be repeated two years later, because the graduates' evaluations will change. Extra work? Yes, but in these days of computers and graduate students (or doctor of ministry candidates) looking for projects, it shouldn't be too difficult to accomplish the task.

Finally, the dean needs to preach and promote integration every opportunity he gets. Any instructor who gives the impression that the students must choose between the theoretical and the practical, between being "scholars" or pastors, should have his knuckles rapped. To ask the immature student to choose between "education" and "training" is to confuse the issue and rob him of the kind of stability he will need in active ministry. He needs both education and training. What God has joined together, let no Ph.D. put asunder.

Dr. Reuel Howe, a specialist in ministerial education, once wrote: "Some faculties resemble a chorus of prima donnas all singing from a different score." Without minimizing any individual discipline, the dean needs to remind each faculty member that the school is preparing pastors for ministry in the local church, and that they must work together to educate and

train young men for the church. And not some abstract
"church" that exists only in the mind of the theologian! The
church we are talking about is made up of real people with real
problems, people who need a shepherd who knows what he is
doing and why he is doing it.

2. *Encourage the instructors to be vitally involved in the local
church.*

This is not easy. A creative teacher is a busy person, and often
he receives invitations to speak in churches and at other schools.
Those invitations satisfy his desire to preach or lecture, they help
the budget, and they give extra exposure to the school. But they
also rob the instructor of his valuable weekends when he might
invest his gifts and experience in a local fellowship.

Another problem: younger pastors sometimes feel threatened
by theological professors sitting in their congregations. A sad
corollary is that sometimes a professor doesn't enjoy sitting in
the pew, listening to a young pastor, and therefore is happy to
have an excuse to be away.

But we have noticed that the instructors who help students the
most are those who believe in the local church and who are
responsible and active members. Even this minimal amount of
involvement helps them present their subjects with a greater emphasis on local church ministry. Every potential faculty member
ought to be interviewed by a few pastors to see what his views
are of the church and the ministry, before he is voted on by the
faculty.

We also believe that each faculty member ought to reflect a
positive view of the church. That is not to suggest that he
whitewash the problems, but only that he share the excitement
of the ministry. If he has not pastored himself, let him beware of
what he says about the church and the ministry. If he has had
painful experiences in the church (and who has not, including
the apostle Paul), then let him admit it and learn to deal positive-
ly with it. Young ministerial students certainly don't need to be
poisoned by negative attitudes. There are enough real problems
on the field without manufacturing imaginary ones in school.

It would help both the students and the churches if the professors would do some writing for the common people for a
change. Granted, each faculty member must grind out his share
of academic literary treasure, but writing only for the experts
rarely accomplishes much good in the churches. A person can
write for a popular audience and still maintain his scholarship.

The students may learn more from a pastor who took his
church from 35 to 300, than from the superstar who has
15 associates and 10 janitors on his staff.

Our Lord's profundity was not based on theological complexity, but on practical simplicity. People understood Him. We need scholarly books, but we can do without bookish scholars who think they are above teaching the common people in the local church. Let our scholars discover how to make truth meaningful to the man on the street, and they will have gone a long way toward making it meaningful and practical to the prospective pastor in their classes.

3. *Rent as much experience and as many minds as you can.*

Wisdom is not going to die with your faculty. Bring in for a week some successful pastors who can share the practical side of ministry with the students. Be sure that you bring in different men with different kinds of ministry. It is easy to be intimidated by gifted men whose success only makes us feel guilty. The pastor who took a church of thirty-five members and built it to three hundred may have more to say to the students than the fellow who has five thousand members and a staff of fifteen associate pastors and ten janitors. For that matter, the pastor who has stayed by the stuff in a smaller church in some rural area may do the men more good than the superstar who probably doesn't even know the names of all his deacons.

And don't forget the people in ministries other than the pastorate: missionaries, journalists, counselors, administrators, chaplains, and so on. While you are at it (and the budget holds out), invite some accomplished laymen and laywomen to visit the classroom and give the "view from the pew." There is a wealth of information and inspiration right in our churches, just waiting to be mined.

Before you reject this idea, think it through: why not bring in a young pastor, with perhaps three years' experience, and let him share his battles and blessings with the students? Not just any pastor, of course, but a man who is positive in his outlook and has learned his lessons with humility and grace. Some young pastors go through the fire and get burned; they become skeptics. Others go through the fire and are purified; they become successes.

We don't know how much money it would take to endow a "visiting lecturer" program, nor do we plan to make the first donation; but it would be wonderful if every school could have one.

4. *Give the students practical training.*

The common complaint seems to be that the new pastor had

no training in how to handle a funeral, how to perform a wedding, how to baptize, how to administer the Lord's Supper, and how to minister to the sick and dying. They may have had lectures, but an hour of experience is worth a year of lectures when it comes to those areas of church life. *Those are the visible ministries in which the new pastor feels very unsure of himself.*

Some professors of practical theology simulate funerals or weddings in the classroom; others take the students on location. One of the best professors we have met expected the students to be able to immerse him successfully—and he stood at six feet and weighed over two hundred pounds! (Even if students don't practice immersion, they ought to know how to administer their own form of baptism with grace and meaning.) Our point is simply this: it ought not to be too difficult for the school to arrange for on-the-spot experience for their students. Supervision is important, of course; otherwise both the student and the school might end up embarrassed.

Instructors in practical theology should never give their students the impression that the classroom notes have adequately prepared them for every challenge of the ministry. Keep reminding them, "There are some things you are simply going to have to learn on the job. I can give you some guidelines and some things to avoid, but they probably won't mean much to you until you are on the field." We believe that fewer graduates will complain if we honestly admit that their academic career does not carry a money-back guarantee.

5. *Help the graduates after they are in a church.*

We have no idea who should do this—the field education director, perhaps, or a special instructor in the practical theology department. It makes no difference, *but it should be done.* Theological education by extension (TEE) is a big thing on the mission field today, but why limit it to missionaries and national pastors? We graduate a student, ship him off to a church, and cut the educational umbilical cord too soon. (His name stays on the mailing list, of course, so that he might be able to be kept informed of campus news and needs.)

Why not have the school sponsor occasional seminars to help update the pastor in areas of ministerial training? Why not free up a good instructor for a couple of weeks of ministry from city to city, meeting with the alumni and teaching them? Would it cost too much to produce an occasional cassette and send it out to the graduates? Include a good chapel message, and perhaps five or ten minutes of meaty material from each of the departments.

Some schools publish an academic journal, but too often it majors on the academic and not the practical. There ought to be balance. We often wished that each department would annually publish a bibliography of the best titles. Surely it wouldn't cost much to mimeograph four or five pages of bibliography.

It is encouraging to see that some schools have planned postordination courses just before or after the annual denominational convention. The pastor can kill two birds with one trip, save money, upgrade his education, and support his denomination.

We may be wrong, but we get the impression that too many schools look at the graduate on the field and ask, "What are you doing for us?" when they ought to be asking, "What more can we do for you?" Our guess is that the schools would receive more loyal support from their alumni if the schools took the servant attitude.

Finally, the schools need to encourage ministerial feedback. We have already suggested an occasional survey, confidential, of course. It might not be a bad idea to invite half a dozen younger pastors to a closed meeting where they can openly discuss their educational needs with a school representative. When faculty members and administrators are bustling about the country in ministry, they ought to contact alumni along the way and discover their needs and listen to their suggestions.

6. *Plan the chapel services for spiritual growth.*

If you are going to have a lecture, then call it a convocation or an assembly, but not chapel. Ministerial students desperately need the worship experience that only chapel can give to the whole academic community. Whoever is in charge of chapel speakers ought to keep in close touch with campus leaders to know what is needed by the students. This may get us into trouble, but we'll say it anyway: not every professor is a preacher, and not every professor needs to speak in chapel. If the professor of Hebrew feels a divine compulsion to discuss the genealogical problems in 1 Chronicles, arrange for a special lecture, but please don't call it chapel. There is a place for instruction that involves the whole campus family, but there is also a place for worship; and the two must not be confused.

We know that the pressures are great, but the chapel service is not the place to parade the pastors whose churches give the most

If the professor of Hebrew wants to lecture on the genealogical problems in 1 Chronicles, let him do it, but don't call it chapel.

to the school. If a man has something to say, give him the opportunity to say it; but don't torture the students just to bless the budget committee. Students are not as dumb as their grades would suggest, and they can tell when a guest speaker is invited because he has a checkbook in his pocket. Is that what we want in our local churches?

There ought to be variety in the chapel worship experience, but not novelty. Not every student responds to a heavy liturgy. At the same time, not every student enjoys singing to the accompaniment of a guitar and recorder. Perhaps the liturgist needs a more informal worship experience, and the "free spirit" needs to understand the beauty of liturgy. So be it.

In chapel, everybody needs to be on the same level. Blessed are faculty members who come as sinners needing grace, as disciples needing teaching, as servants needing direction! Blessed are those students who don't try to impress each other as they worship God! Blessed is that campus family that can unite heart and voice in praise to God, forgetting academic distinctions, receiving from God the grace needed for life and ministry!

Those are our modest suggestions. None of them seems too difficult to adopt. We don't guarantee they will work, but we do have high hopes that they will.

Thanks for listening!

Some Books That Have Helped Us

This is not a list of the "best books," because we don't know what the "best books" are for you in your particular situation. These are books that have helped us along the way and that perhaps may help you. We have mentioned others in the text that are not repeated here.

Bayly, Joseph. *The Last Thing We Talk About*. Elgin, Ill.: David C. Cook, 1973.

Blackwood, Andrew W. *The Growing Minister*. Nashville: Abingdon, 1960.

_____. *The Funeral*. Grand Rapids: Baker, 1972.

_____. *Planning a Year's Pulpit Work*. Grand Rapids: Baker, 1975.

Bridges, Charles. *The Christian Ministry*. London: Banner of Truth, 1958.

Brooks, Phillips. *Lectures on Preaching*. Grand Rapids: Baker, 1978.

Daane, James. *Preaching with Confidence: A Theological Essay on the Power of the Pulpit*. Grand Rapids: Eerdmans, 1980.

Escott, Harry, ed. *The Cure of Souls: An Anthology of P. T. Forsyth's Practical Writings*. Grand Rapids: Eerdmans, 1971.

Farmer, H. H. *The Servant of the Word*. Philadelphia: Fortress, 1942.

Getz, Gene. *Sharpening the Focus of the Church*. Chicago: Moody, 1976.

Howkins, Kenneth. *The Challenge of Religious Studies*. Downers Grove, Ill.: Inter-Varsity, 1972.

Jefferson, Charles. *The Building of the Church*. Grand Rapids: Baker, 1969.

————. *The Minister as Shepherd*. Fort Washington, Pa.: Christian Literature Crusade.

Kepler, Thomas S., ed. *The Table Talk of Martin Luther*. Grand Rapids: Baker, 1979.

————. *Treasury of Great Devotional Writings*. Grand Rapids: Baker, n.d.

Lloyd-Jones, D. Martyn. *Preaching and Preachers*. London: Hodder and Stoughton, 1971.

Packer, J. I. *Knowing God*. Downers Grove, Ill.: Inter-Varsity, 1973.

Phillips, J. B. *Your God Is Too Small*. New York: Macmillan, n.d.

Quayle, William. *The Pastor-Preacher*. Grand Rapids: Baker, 1979.

Sanders, J. Oswald. *A Spiritual Clinic*. Chicago: Moody, 1958.

————. *Spiritual Maturity*. Chicago: Moody, 1962.

————. *Spiritual Leadership*. Chicago: Moody, 1967.

Stalker, James. *The Preacher and His Models*. Grand Rapids: Baker, 1967.

Stewart, James. *A Faith to Proclaim*. London: Hodder and Stoughton, 1953.

Stott, John R. W. *The Preacher's Portrait*. Grand Rapids: Eerdmans, 1961.

Tozer, A. W. *The Knowledge of the Holy*. New York: Harper & Row, 1961.

————. *The Pursuit of God*. New York: Harper & Row, 1978.

Turnbull, Ralph. *A Minister's Obstacles*. Grand Rapids: Baker, 1976.

————. *A Minister's Opportunities*. Grand Rapids: Baker, 1979.

Woodbridge, John, ed., et al. *The Gospel in America: Themes in the Story of America's Evangelicals*. Grand Rapids: Zondervan, 1979.

Of course, we have been greatly helped by the writings of C. S. Lewis, Charles Haddon Spurgeon, George Morrison, and the various "greats" of preaching history. For a survey of great preachers and their ministries, see *Walking with the Giants, Listening to the Giants,* and *Giant Steps,* all by Warren W.

Wiersbe and published by Baker Book House, Grand Rapids, Michigan. For a selection of classic sermons from great preachers, see *A Treasury of the World's Great Sermons,* edited by Warren W. Wiersbe and published by Kregel Publishers, Grand Rapids, Michigan.